COMING TO LAND

in a troubled world

COMING TO LAND

in a troubled world

essays by
Peter Forbes
Kathleen Dean Moore
Scott Russell Sanders

foreword by
Will Rogers

edited by
Helen Whybrow

A Center for Land and People Book
The Trust for Public Land
San Francisco, California

The editor and publisher wish to thank the following writers and publishers for
permission to reprint copyrighted material:

Excerpts from "A Field Guide to the Sixth Extinction," by Niles Eldridge and "To
Whom it May Concern," by Jared Diamond both copyright © 1999 by *The New York
Times*. Excerpts from *Coming Back to Life*, copyright © Joanna Macy 1998. Excerpt
from *The Phenomenon of Man* copyright © 1965 by Pierre Teilhard de Chardin.
Excerpt from "A Jewish Time Capsule," copyright by Rabbi Malka Drucker.

Book design by Peter Holm, Sterling Hill Production
Cover photo by John Rosenthal
Back cover photo by Peter Forbes

Printed in the United States of America
Printed with soy based ink on recycled paper by Queen City Printers

A Center for Land and People Book
published by
The Trust for Public Land
116 New Montgomery Street
San Francisco, CA 94105
415.495.4014
www.tpl.org

ISBN 0-9672806-9-9
9 8 7 6 5 4 3 2 1

CONTENTS

ACKNOWLEDGMENTS

I AM EVER grateful for the hard work of my friends and colleagues at the Trust for Public Land (TPL), who collectively are the crucible for these ideas. Their commitment to expanding the role of land and nature in our civil society is the primary reason I put pen to paper.

This is the fourth and final book in a series on "Re-Thinking the Promise of Land Conservation." Each of these books has been deeply informed and inspired by the members of a remarkable advisory council for the Center for Land and People who met on three different occasions to discuss and contribute to all of the themes of this book. I feel an enormous debt of gratitude to these individuals for what they have given to me, to TPL, and to the practice of land conservation: William Cronon, Michael Dorsey, Dianne Dumanoski, Torri Estrada, Jan Flora, Eric Freyfogle, Tony Hiss, Kurt Hoelting, Gary Paul Nabhan, David Orr, Michael Pollan, Anne Whiston Spirn, Mary Evelyn Tucker, Mark Walters, Scott Russell Sanders, and Alvin Warren.

The lion's share of what I do as a conservationist, photographer, and writer is simply to interpret and re-tell what has earlier been given to me. The purpose of my essay is to share that borrowed wisdom. People with whom I've shared meaningful conversations about the ideas in this book, whether in a kayak, around a campfire, in a conference room, or on a hike, include: Mark Coleman, Bill Coperthwaite, Grove Burnett, John Elder, Tovar Cerruli, Virginia Farley, Chuck Matthei, Wendy Johnson, Gil Livingston, Will Rogers, Trebbe Johnson, Dan Neumeyer, Bob Perschel, Sandra Tassel, Hans Schoepflin, Mary O'Brien, Nancy Shea,

John Saltmarsh, Carla High Eagle, and Terry Tempest Williams. Their intuition and wisdom is visible in these pages.

I want to thank three people whose work has had a particular influence on my conception of Whole Thinking. I thank Derrick Jensen for giving us *Listening to the Land* and for his honesty and truth-telling as revealed in his books and lectures. I thank Thomas Berry, whose work has long inspired my actions and whom I met for the first time during the writing of this essay. His clarity, warmth, and dedication set an important benchmark for all of us. Joanna Macy's influence on the ideas in this book is quite obvious. I was able to spend four days with Joanna during the writing of this essay and I hold dear that experience as a testament to the contribution that one person can make to an entire culture of activism.

I also want to thank several others whose written and spoken words have helped me this year to be less blind: Theodore Roethke, Teilhard de Chardin, David Ehrenfeld, Michael Mead, Niles Eldridge, Jared Diamond, Barbara Kingsolver, Rabbi Malka Drucker, R. D. Laing, Robert Michael Pyle, Vandana Shiva, E. O. Wilson, Gary Paul Nabhan, and Jack Turner.

The University of New Hampshire very kindly gave me the opportunity to reflect on Rachel Carson when they invited me to give one of their Dunphy lectures. My thoughts on Aldo Leopold and Scott Nearing first came into focus as a lecture I gave in June 2002 at the Stratton Foundation's Symposium on Scott and Helen Nearing's Vermont Experiment. Many of the ideas that I call Whole Thinking were presented, feverishly, for my land conservation colleagues at the 2002 National Land Trust Rally in Austin, Texas.

The Park Foundation and the Compton Foundation provided funding to make this book possible. I am deeply grateful to Alicia Gomer Wittink, Suzanne Michelle, and Edith Eddy for their faith in me.

I want to pay tribute to Julianne Newton, whose thinking and influence are felt on every page of my essay. Julianne has contributed her significant insights to all four of the books in this series as a researcher, collaborator, reviewer, and fellow writer. Julianne's scholarship, activism, and great belief in the health of people and the land have made these books immeasurably better. My colleagues at the Center for Land and People, Kate Williams and Cara Robecheck, also contributed a great deal to moving this work and this thinking forward, and to them I owe a great deal.

Lastly, Helen Whybrow has served as the editor and co-creator of all four books. Without her insights on conservation and language, her professionalism and dedication, these books simply would not exist. To Helen and Willow, with whom I share this land, I offer my deepest affections.

Peter Forbes
Knoll Farm
Fayston, Vermont

FOREWORD

Will Rogers

PRESIDENT, THE TRUST FOR PUBLIC LAND

IN MY LEADERSHIP role in the conservation community, I am determined to focus on the joy and hope and possibility that land-and-people conservation holds for our society. I am committed to telling the positive stories about what can happen when individuals and communities affirm the most profound human values through conservation projects that honor the human and natural worlds together. I choose to affirm the values of love, fairness, home, and a healthy natural world that are possible through the connection between people and place, people and nature. But often this "glass half-full" attitude does not come easily.

As a nation—as a species—we are having to repair the damage caused by our poor choices. We are learning the hard way that our resources are not infinite and that a healthy sustainable society depends on healthy natural systems. We are learning that what we do to the land we do to ourselves. We are learning the hard way that we can't afford to ignore the health and well being of our fellow species any more than we can afford to ignore each other. When it comes to relearning how to live and what matters most, I find great hope in the promise of conservation—to affirm, restore, and heal relationships with people and nature. I am buoyed by the commitment and spirit I see within this country's community of dedicated conservationists—in the face of daunting challenges.

The essays in this collection speak to the power and importance of our relationship with the land and with nature and give us both hope and a recipe for a healthier future.

Those of us who labor with the nuts and bolts of the place-saving business, dealing with the myriad political, financial, legal, and stewardship challenges that define land conservation in this country, need a regular reminder of the power of this work and how much it can contribute to a healthier society and a healthier planet. We need to remember that this work is not about conserving places, it is about conserving people and our fellow species in the web of life. It is about helping people find a different way to live.

Land conservation and the strength of our relationships with the places we care about can provide a powerful entry point in the struggle to reverse the bad decisions we have made as a society. But to capture the benefits of land-and-people conservation, we also need to set aside conservation's usual benchmarks and measurements and ask ourselves, What really matters? Is it acres or fair market value? Is it membership statistics or fundraising results? Is it new legislation or better zoning and planning? All of these are important. Yet none of them speaks to why we do this work.

When we begin to measure the success of our land conservation work in children's smiles in parks and gardens, moments of inspiration in a remote and powerful landscape, pumpkins harvested at a local farm, the glow of health from walking or running neighborhood trails and greenways, or the flexing of our sense of wonder in the presence of nature close to home, then we will know the impact of our work. When our sense of accomplishment expands to include these difficult to measure intangibles, we will be living and working with the promise of conservation.

The work that we at TPL and other conservation organizations are doing to expand our thinking about conservation and its promise for a healthier society is very much an exploration. We invite you to join us in this important effort. Please share with us your thoughts and ideas for how we might use what we know to increase our impact in making this a better world. Visit us at www.tpl.org and add your thoughts to this important discussion.

LANDING

Kathleen Dean Moore

I HAD BEEN away for many days, sitting behind glass walls in one airport waiting room after another, cold and fidgety in a black plastic chair, uneasy under the grim eyes of security guards. With all the other lonely, tired, anxious people, I stood in lines with my identification in my hand. Then we were grinding through clouds thirty-five thousand feet above the earth. The noise was overwhelming and so was the silence of strangers crowded side by side, wincing when their elbows touched. I was startled when the flight attendant announced we would be landing.

"What did she say?" I asked the man next to me.

"We'll be landing soon—that's what she said." Seatback in an upright position, tray table locked, I seized on those words. *Land* is a noun, a solid, a place you come home to. *Land* is a set of relationships—ecosystems, hydrological cycles, ocean currents, neighborhoods and nitrogen cycles, and the energy that flows among them. But *land* is also a verb, an action that people sometimes take: To land is to come into contact again (finally, blessedly) with the actual earth, a place that welcomes you, nourishes you, protects you, lifts you with relief. Suddenly, I wanted to land more than anything else in the world.

We have been away for many centuries, we people of the western industrialized nations. We have built a culture on the mistaken assumption that human beings are independent of one another and of the places and systems of the earth. And so the mass of us lead lives of quiet separation, cutting ourselves off from the ecological and cultural communities that sustain us. The mass of us live apart from our parents and their memories, from our children and their grown-up hopes, from the sources of our food and energy and water, from our neighbors, from the wind and rain. Behind locked gates and Thermopane windows, in front of computer screens and air conditioning units, we might as well be suspended in the sky, for all the contact we have with the actual earth. The separation hurts: Isolated, uneasy, we crave something we can never buy and grieve for a loss we can't name.

As I have traveled, I have met many people who are trying to end cultural and economic alienation from the natural world. They are actively engaged in the work of "landing." Coming back to their places, they imagine, create, and celebrate sustaining, joyous relationships among people and the land. Volunteers flood a marsh or plant willows along a stream. The Trust for Public Land raises a farmer's market in an abandoned railroad yard or stops a Wal-Mart from swallowing a farm. A mother plants blue camas in the backyard or teaches her son to tell a varied thrush from a robin by the lilt of its song. But all these efforts are piecemeal and futile, if we aren't able to do the real work of reconciliation, which is telling the truth.

We have learned some things about truth from the last sad century, and we learn them again as this new century makes its bloody start: Without the lies that alienate us from our enemies and make carnage seem necessary and good, wars of aggression are impossible. Reconciliation begins only when people bring themselves to tell the truth about their enemies, all members of the same human family, and about the damage war does to the earth, their home, as it is home to their foes.

In just the same way, alienation from the land has allowed us to wage war against the water, the air, the fertile soil. We who depend on the life-sustaining systems of the earth can act in ways that harm them, only if we successfully convince ourselves, against all evidence, that the damage we do to the land is justified, or necessary, or inconsequential. So we buy into a set of illusions about our supposed separation from the land, and convince ourselves that our acts are conveniently disconnected from their consequences. Until we begin to tell the truth about the intimacy of our relation to natural places, I see no reason to hope that the work of reconciliation with the land can begin.

What are the lies that isolate us? What are the illusions of separation and self-sufficiency that allow us to think of ourselves as sensible people, while we make decisions that sabotage the ecological systems on which our lives depend? Here are just a few:

Today / Tomorrow

Caught up in the moment, we act as if today were somehow disconnected from tomorrow, as if we floated in a holy present, untethered from what has come before us, unaffected by and certainly not responsible for what will happen next.

Surely, I say to myself, no one believes it's possible to sever the connection between past, present, and future. But how else could people who love their children act in ways that diminish or destroy the world in which their children will live? How else could voters allow industry to endlessly mine the land and the lakes and the seas, liquidating the earth's assets, extinguishing species forever, holding this great going-out-of-business sale, and forget that it is our children who will be left standing in the empty store?

As we disregard the future, time spirals through us. The presences and absences—what remains and what will never be again—are a result of decisions made by the people who came before us. Our children will live in the world we are creating today, as we bustle about, planting the seeds of cancer and the seeds of hollyhocks, tall and green. Will we cut the last ancient forests and empty the oceans? Will we foul the desert with uranium-tipped missiles and litter the arctic with discarded oil-drilling rigs? Will we drench strawberry fields with Diazinon and lace the spinach with 2,4-D? Will we undermine the power of antibiotics and create new weeds that can never be controlled?

We can look back at our parents' decisions—about pesticides, radioactive waste, PCB's, the grand and fatal dams—and say that perhaps our parents didn't understand the consequences of their acts. When our children look back on our decisions, they won't allow us that excuse.

God knows, it's easy enough to delude ourselves that the damage done to the earth's natural systems has nothing to do with us. Our language invites us to dodge responsibility. "The species went extinct," we say. "The forest was clear-cut." "The river was dammed." "The last fish was caught." "The aquifer was contaminated." Always the passive voice, the sentence where the agent has gone missing. The chronicle of loss is sad and shameful enough, but the grammar is terrifying.

The fact is that species don't go extinct, the way little pigs go to market; with some exceptions, human decisions drive species to extinction. Trees don't sever themselves cleanly at the knees and keel over; rather, humans pay other humans to go into the forest, rev up their chainsaws, and cut down the trees: the squealing saw, the crashing branches, the flying debris, the frantic cawing of crows. We—you and I, by our decisions—are causal agents in the harm done the natural systems of the earth.

These truths aren't easy truths. It's painful, the switch from "What is happening to the world?" to "What am I doing to the world?" But this kind of truth-telling—acknowledging that we are complicit today in the degradation of the world our children will live in tomorrow—opens a door to reconciliation and renewal. If we understand that our decisions create the future, then we can imagine a different set of decisions, and thus a different future. This creates the possibility of choice—commitment to a set of life-giving values that are the foundation of new communities of renewal.

My university colleague, Frank Lake, returns to his home along the Klamath River each year to join his Yurok people for the Dance of World Renewal. He believes that the land creates the people, as a mother creates her children, and brings the rain and salmon. He also understands that people create the land. They plant willows in the lowlands and renew the meadows with prairie fires. Or people cut forests on steep slopes and rip-rap the streams—this happens too. For better or worse, people and the land are co-creators of the future. They share the responsibility for determining what the next years will bring.

So the Yurok families come together each year in their town, landing in that place from colleges and cities and ranch houses and fishing ports. It's a reconciliation, quite literally, a coming together again, a re-union of people and land. Singing and dancing, they acknowledge the human responsibility to create a world in which their children can thrive.

As soon as I got home from the airport after my long time away, I rode my bike to the Farmer's Market by the river in my town. Like the Dance of World Renewal in Frank's hometown, this gathering in my hometown is a kind of reconciliation, a coming together again of past and future, people and the land.

There were buckets of flowers, the second week in June—yellow lilies, peonies, field daisies—and rows of tomato plants in pots. A father pushed a stroller past an abundance of lettuce, while his baby gnawed a strawberry, dribbling juice into the folds of her chin. As a fiddler played, a little boy danced, embracing a bundle of carrots. People moved slowly past oysters piled high on ice, stopping to talk with friends whose arms overflowed with leaf lettuce and sweet basil and tiny yellow potatoes just dug from the ground. Spinach in great heaps spilled over garlic sprouts under striped awnings, and behind it all, the river flashed between trees shiny with new leaves. The music, the quiet conversations, the smell of green onions and mock-orange—this world as it once was, the world as it can be again—flooded me with a joy that I am still trying to understand.

Near / Far

A second delusion is that the nearby places where we live are ecologically and culturally separable from what is far away—other peoples' neighborhoods or "Nature" out on a mountaintop somewhere. This allows us to believe that it is possible to safeguard one's own backyard without regard for the distant places, and the reverse: that it is possible to safeguard distant beloved places while the close-in neighborhoods collapse around us. On the contrary, the ecosystems that sustain us are linked in beautiful and complex ways to each other, to economic and social systems, and to the land. Living in this interlocking whole, we need to find our own integrity, a moral wholeness that holds us to the same standards of care for the land, no matter where we are.

Whenever I fly toward home, the plane drops below clouds that soak the foothills of the Willamette River valley where I live. I look down on a tufted landscape of clear-cuts and tree plantations. Human commerce has skinned and sectioned the hills, slicing them along political lines, property lines, fence lines, power lines. Lines dividing wilderness and corporate land, public land and private property, subdivision and nature reserve, nature and culture, run straight and square across the curving hills.

The moral distinctions are every bit as visible on the mountainsides. Far from home, there are odd patches of wilderness

ethic, where people feel a strong obligation to do no harm.
Then come wide swaths of utilitarian ethic, where the land (the
water, the forests, the city street, the night sky, the schoolyard,
the railroad station) is treated as a commodity, and people are
careless of it, or disdainful, and push it around or use it up
willy-nilly. Close to home are square, green homeplaces, where
people care for the land as if it were their child, cherishing it
and keeping it well.

But in the earth's great systems—the hydrological cycles, the
patterns of weather, the spread of disease, the migrations of
birds and peoples, genetic drift, continental drift, pesticide
drift, drift nets—there is no distinction between far and near.
A surveyor can draw a line around a wilderness area or a subdivision, but boundaries do not hold water. When storm winds
billow in, every boundary is hidden in fog that dampens stumps
and forests without distinction. Carbon dioxide doesn't stay in
a parking lot. Plutonium has no respect for a chain-link fence.
Diseases born on the far side of the earth walk onto planes and
disembark at LaGuardia or Hong Kong. And all the while, oxygen created in lowland marshes drifts toward cities on rising
winds, as fresh water filtered in great forests runs downhill to
the glass pitchers in the old-folks' home.

Near or far, it's all one interdependent, unfathomable thing.
So the moral distinctions fall away too. What sense does it
make to live by different ethics in different places, in a world
so intimately connected?

If the land is all one homeplace, then we should treat it as
thoughtfully and carefully as we treat our homes. The ecological oneness of near and far requires a moral integrity as well, a
vision of the possibility of living in a caring relationship with all
land, of walking anywhere on earth with the same gratitude and
respect.

This evening, my husband and I will walk down to the river,

carrying our supper. As people gradually gather, we will sit at picnic tables by the skate park, in the shadow of the graffiti-wall where teenagers spray-paint fierce self-portraits. Sharing binoculars, we will watch the big brown bats leave their roosts and fly off over the river to feed. We will talk about the bats, meet some people we haven't known before, be astonished and glad, and then we will walk home through warm air filtered by lichens and the lungs of strangers. We will climb into bed while the moon rises over the town, as it rose over the blowing wilderness, as it will rise over the sea. And we will fall asleep while sea fog condenses on broad lawns and drips from the eaves of the Super 8 Motel.

Us / Them

There's a great bustle of work in my neighborhood this morning. The neighbor to the southeast is tearing out what once was a jungle of laurel, rhododendron, and the shrub the children call the 'snowball bush.' This has prompted the neighbor to the northeast to build a fence. I can smell the fresh pine boards, but I can't see the fence through my beloved laurel hedge, which is twenty feet tall and ten feet wide.

Listening to the thwack of hammer on damp wood, I think about a third dichotomy: the separation of individual well being from the well being of others, whether human or nonhuman. This allows us to believe that an individual can find health and happiness in isolation, with no regard for the health and happiness of other people or the health of the land. The illusion of separation, us versus them, deludes us on every scale—not just individuals, but cities, nations, religions, multi-national corporations, each devising a plot to thrive alone, while around it, ecosystems are destroyed and people are denied the basic means of subsistence, in lives without health and beauty and safety.

On an individual scale, I have seen people search all their

lives for what would make them happy and whole—perpetual seekers, not sure what they are looking for, but endlessly searching, on the internet, in catalogs, at the mall—never thinking to look out a window or knock on a neighbor's door. We are creatures who crave connection to other people and to places that hold our hopes and memories. The hurtful things we do (the endless travel, the huge houses, the shopping, shopping, shopping) may be a kind of grief work, a way to fill the emptiness that hollows out a life that has no meaningful connection to others and to the land.

The same despair seems to mark our national life. Suddenly obsessed with security in a time of war, the nation debates about what makes a person safe. With sentries, walls, security checkpoints, border guards, and gated communities, to isolate oneself from others, particularly from others who are in need or in danger—is this the way to assure personal well being? Or does long-term individual safety depend on strong relationships within communities where people thrive in harmony with each other and the natural world?

Obsessed with health in a time of death, the nation debates about what makes a person healthy. With antibiotics, aggressive medical intervention, radical mastectomies, amputations, and quarantines, to fight against the invasions of organisms that would do us harm—is this the only way to assure personal health? Or does long-term health depend also on supportive communities and healthy biocultural landscapes—fertile, clean places free of contaminants that poison our cells and foul our lungs?

Obsessed with wealth, can a person, or a nation, or a multinational corporation secure prosperity for itself without regard for the well being of all those creatures, human or not, who breathe the same air? What a futility, this grinding wheel of isolation and insecurity. In self-imposed exile from sources of comfort and fulfillment, a person (a nation, a corporation) grasps after wealth and power, chewing up ecosystems and social systems, creating injustice and enemies. A quite sensible fear of the enemies they have made and the instability they have created triggers a frantic search for security. But without a healthy, supportive community, where will anyone find security but in wealth and power? And so it sadly, disastrously goes.

Centuries ago, Plato wrote that democracies cannot last; they inevitably turn into oligarchies, the rule by the wealthy few, as more and more wealth and power concentrate in fewer hands. Oligarchies, he wrote, disintegrate into anarchy. For years, I didn't believe him. I believe him now. And I believe as well that Plato's only mistake was to fail to warn us how quickly an oligarchy will destroy itself, by destroying the ecosystems and social systems on which its wealth and power depend. The greatest challenge of the environmental movement in this decade is to understand and make others understand the connection between social injustice, insecurity, and despoliation of the natural world.

Humans / Nature

Finally, the most disastrous self-deception, the idea that human beings are separate from and superior to the rest of the natural world, and the equally disastrous corollary: We can destroy our habitats without destroying ourselves.

As we begin to understand instead that humans are seamlessly connected, are kin, to the natural world, then we may begin to act in caring ways toward the earth and its inhabitants. This is a matter both of pragmatic self-interest, sustaining the systems that sustain us, and of moral obligation, honoring and caring for our relations.

Jack Forbes, a Powhatan-Ren'pe scholar and a poet, pointed out how much humans are of the natural world. "You can cut off my hands," he told my students, "and I will still live. You can cut off my ears, and I will still live. Gouge out my eyes, and I will live. Cut off my legs, my hair, my nose, and I will still live. But if you cut off my air, I will die. If you take away the water, I will die. So why do I think that my hands and my eyes are more a part of me than the water and the air?"

How complicated and layered and open-ended is this relation of humans to all of natural creation, this kinship, this beautiful, bewildering family. First, there is the kinship of common substance. Like a cottonwood tree or a neighborhood cat, I am carbon atoms spun through time, arranged and rearranged in patterns. Break my pattern down to atoms, and I can scarcely be distinguished from the stars.

Second, there is the kinship of common origins. All of us human beings, friends and enemies, have one or another of the same hominid mother, nursing her baby with her back against a tree. Perhaps she understood, in ways we have forgotten, her origins in the same expanse of time and savannah that gave rise to the jackalberry trees and termites around her.

Third, there is the kinship of interdependence. I feed my son who plants cedars that filter the air that pumps through the heart of the son who fills my life with love. Which of us could live without the other?

And fourth, the kinship of a common fate. What happens to any of us—blue-green algae or galaxies, philosophers or Douglas firs—happens to us all. Because the earth, its air and water and all its creatures are part of a single, complicated system, there is no way to separate the human and nonhuman costs of habitat degradation. Harm done to the natural environment is also direct damage to humans, violence against the necessary conditions of biological and spiritual thriving.

This kinship has moral consequences. "All ethics," wrote conservationist Aldo Leopold, "rests on a single premise: that the individual is a member of a community of interdependent parts," a community that includes "soils, water, plants, animals, or collectively, the land." People value connections to the natural places that create and sustain us: The sudden awareness of kinship to the earth fills us with joy. This is what I felt when I flew home from so far away, landed, and made my way to the farmers' market, the piled carrots grown from the same soil as my neighbors and children.

Moral obligations grow from relationships. If we are of the land, and if we care about and depend on our connections to it, then we ought to act in ways that nurture, enhance, and celebrate healthy webs of connection with the land and all the members of the biotic community.

Landing is what we need to do in this time and place—the sudden slowing, the jolt of reconnection, the relief of coming again into a meaningful connection with the solid earth. But that's not to say that landing is an easy thing. Landing makes me edgy as hell; I know it's the second most dangerous part of any flight, next to taking off. But it's not the fear of crash-landing that shakes me, but the fear of what I will find when I come home.

For years and years, I flew to Ohio for reunions with my family. Landing was a festive time, when all the relatives milled around the gate, and the hugs blocked the exit until a laughing guard shooed us away, and we walked together down the concourse, a dozen people arm-in-arm. But each year, fewer and fewer people met my flights. My mother became too sick to travel to the airport. The cousins moved away. My grandmother died. Finally it was only my father who came to meet me, even when he had to push down the concourse in a wheelchair. And then not even he came. I walked down the concourse alone and climbed into a taxi that delivered me to a lonely, diminished father and a house filled with pain.

And so it is sometimes, with coming back to the land. Each year less and less remains of what we love in the land. In the town where I grew up, a parking lot for a sausage restaurant destroyed the meadow where we wove necklaces with Queen-Anne's lace. The swampy place where the two rivers meet is now a soccer field. An apartment complex squats where frogs used to sing. I could go on and on: What limit is there to the human ability to transmogrify the dewy, bird-graced, dapple-lighted places into hot pavement? Coming back to the land can be a time of sorrow and regret.

Sometimes I think that we who love the land grieve for the loss of wild places in ways that are hard to distinguish from the ways we grieve for the loss of a beloved person. The intensity of sorrow may be less, but conservationists make the same journey through the stages of grief that psychologist Elisabeth Kübler-Ross described.

The first stage is denial. Maybe it's not too late to save the salmon, or the grandfather forest, or the ivory-billed woodpecker (choose one). Maybe carbon dioxide poisoning is good for forests. Maybe global warming is just a protest-industry fund-raising scam. Maybe arsenic in water doesn't hurt anybody.

The second stage is anger. What kind of person would pave a frog pond? Who would throw the switch that releases lead into the air? What level of hell is reserved for the corporate scientist who designs new poisons for food, carpets, playground equipment? Who sent bunker oil through a pristine fjord in a single-hulled ship? Whoever it is, may Mother Earth grab him in one rocky hand and hold him underwater until he no longer bubbles.

Then, bargaining. How well we conservationists know this part of the progression of grief. Dam this river, flood the ancient canyons, but save this free-running stream. Build your ugly subdivision, but put in bike paths and make a park beside the creek. Bulldoze this marsh, but dig a wet place by the freeway. Bargaining, trading, compromising, accomplishing what we can, ignoring what we can't, we celebrate any small victory in a losing war.

Fourth? The fourth step is depression. Deep enough to drown in.

The fifth stage of grief is acceptance. The person we mourn will not return. Nor will the extinct birds or the ancient mossy forests—not in this place, not in our lifetimes. There is a certain peace in acceptance, in going on with life in a diminished world. But for the conservationist, for the person who loves the beleaguered world, there has to be a sixth step, beyond sorrow, beyond acceptance.

I don't know what the particular shape of the sixth stage will be, but I know it will require creative acts of commitment—acts of imagining and choosing. We may not be able to *find* much wholeness in our poor, patched-together world. But that doesn't mean that we can't *create* new wholes, bringing today and tomorrow, near and far, us and them, human and nature together into living, sustaining biocultural communities.

We know what it means to land—the final approach, the drop, the bump, the shuddering surge before the noisy slowing. After the longest time, the doors open and the air of home rushes in, carrying a sudden sense of safety and the prospect of joining again the people and places we love. We can taste on the wind the life that we are capable of living, learn again the happiness that comes from caring for people and caring for places, and accept the challenge of reconciliation, bringing together again what has been apart for a very long time.

KATHLEEN DEAN MOORE is Distinguished Professor of Philosophy at Oregon State University and the author of *Riverwalking*, and *Holdfast*. Her latest book, *The Island Paradox*, from which ideas and material in this essay are drawn, will be published by Milkweed Editions in spring 2004.

A CONSERVATIONIST'S MANIFESTO

Scott Russell Sanders

1. The work of conservation is inspired by wonder, gratitude, reason, and love. We need all of these emotions and faculties to do the work well. But the first impulse is love—love for wild and settled places, for animals and plants, for people living now and those yet to come, for the creations of human hands and minds.

2. In our time, the work of conservation is also inspired by a sense of loss. We feel keenly the spreading of deserts, clearcutting of forests, extinction of species, poisoning of air and water and soil, disruption of climate, and the consequent suffering of countless people. We recognize that Earth's ability to support life is being degraded by a burgeoning human population, extravagant consumption, and reckless technology. The most reckless technology is the machinery of war, which drains away vast amounts of labor and resources, distracts nations from the needs of their citizens, and wreaks havoc on both land and people.

3. The scale of devastation caused by human activity is unprecedented, and it is accelerating, spurred on by a global system of nation-states battling for advantage, and by an economic system addicted to growth and waste. So the work of conservation becomes ever more urgent. To carry on in the midst of so much loss, we must have faith that people working together can reverse the destructive

trends. We must believe that our species is capable of imagining and achieving fundamental changes in our way of life.

4. Even while we respond to emergencies—keeping oil rigs out of wildlife refuges, saving farms from bulldozers—we must also work for the long-term healing of land, people, and culture. Conservation means not only protecting the relatively unscathed natural areas that survive, but also mending, so far as possible, what has been damaged. We can't undo all of the damage. No amount of effort or money, for example, will restore the roughly 50 percent of the world's coral reefs that are now dying or dead because of pollution, dynamiting, and ocean warming. But we can replant forests and prairies, reflood wetlands, clean up rivers, transform brownfields into parks, return species to their native habitats, and leave the wildest of places alone to heal themselves.

5. The cost of such restoration is so great, and the results so uncertain, that we should make every effort to prevent the damage in the first place. Although skillful work may help, all healing ultimately depends on the self-renewing powers of nature. Our task is to understand and cooperate with those powers as fully as we can.

6. Conservation should aim to preserve the integrity and diversity of natural systems, from the local watershed to the biosphere, rather than to freeze any given landscape into some ideal condition. Nature is never fixed, but in constant flow. If we try to halt that flow, we may cause more harm than good, and we are certain to waste our energies. When we speak of ecological health, we do not refer to a static condition, but to a dynamic web of relationships. We ourselves are woven into that web, every cell in our bodies, every thought in our minds.

7. Lands, rivers, and oceans are healthy when they sustain the full range of ecological processes. Healthy wild land filters its own water and builds its own soil, as in ancient forests or unplowed prairies. Agricultural land is healthy when it is gaining rather than losing fertility, and when it leaves room for other species in woodlots and hedgerows. Whether wild or cultivated, healthy lands and seas are diverse, resilient, and beautiful.

8. Healthy villages and cities are also diverse, resilient, and beautiful. No human settlement can flourish apart from a flourishing landscape, nor can a family or an individual thrive in a ruined place. Likewise, no landscape can flourish so long as the inhabitants of that place lack the basics of a decent life—safe and adequate food and water, secure shelter, access to education and medical care, protection from violence, chances for useful work, and hope for the future.

9. Concern for ecological health and concern for social justice are therefore inseparable. Anyone who pits the good of land against the good of people, as if we could choose between them, is either ignorant or deceitful.

10. Justice and compassion require us to use Earth's bounty sparingly and to share it out equitably. For citizens in the richest nations, this will mean living more simply, satisfying our needs rather than our wants. For citizens in the poorest nations, this will mean satisfying basic needs in ways that are least harmful to the land. For all nations, this will mean slowing the growth in human population—an effort already underway with some success—and it will mean eventually reducing our numbers until we are once more in balance with Earth's carrying capacity.

11. A concern for justice also requires us to provide for everyone, regardless of location or income or race, the opportunity for contact with healthy land. All people deserve the chance to breathe clean air and drink clean water, to meet birds and butterflies, to walk among wildflowers, to glimpse the primal world of big trees and untamed rivers, rocky shores and starry nights.

12. Justice to other species requires us to preserve habitats where our fellow creatures may dwell. Through farming, fishing, hunting, and the harvesting of trees and other plants, we already use nearly half of Earth's biological production. We have no right to claim so much, let alone more. Simple gratitude to other species for the nourishment, instruction, companionship, and inspiration they have given us should be reason enough to fight for their survival. Concern for our own survival should lead us to protect the web of life by preserving a vast and robust range of habitats, from backyard gardens and schoolyard prairies to marine sanctuaries and deep wilderness.

13. Justice to future generations requires us to pass along the beauty and bounty of Earth undiminished. Our politics, economy, and media betray an almost infantile fixation on the present moment, seeking or selling instant gratification, oblivious to history. We need to develop a culture worthy of adults, one that recognizes our actions have consequences. If we take more than we need from the riches of the planet, if we drain aquifers, squander topsoil, or fish the seas bare, we are stealing from our children. If we fill dumps with toxic waste, fill barrels with radioactive debris, spew poisons into the atmosphere and oceans, we will leave our descendants a legacy of grief. Conservation aims to avoid causing harm to our children, or their children, or to any children ever.

14. Whatever else we teach our children, we owe them an ecological education. We need to give them time outdoors, where they can meet and savor the world that humans have not made—pill bugs on a sidewalk, a swarm of tadpoles in a puddle, a tree for climbing, a sky aflame with sunset, a kiss of wind. Such contact gives promise of a lifelong joy in the presence of nature. By the time they finish school, children who have received an ecological education know in their bones that the well-being of people depends on the well-being of Earth, from the neighborhood to the watershed to the planet.

15. Whether children or adults, we take care of what we love. Our sense of moral obligation arises from a feeling of kinship. The illusion of separation—between human and nonhuman, rich and poor, black and white, native and stranger—is the source of our worst behavior. The awareness of kinship is the source of our best behavior.

16. Just as all people belong to the same family, regardless of the surface differences that seem to divide us, so all living things are interrelated. We depend on the integrity and services of Earth's natural systems, from enzymes in our bellies to currents in the oceans, from bees pollinating fruits to ozone blocking ultraviolet light.

17. The integrity we perceive in nature is our own birthright. We swim in the one and only stream of life. By recognizing that we are part of this vast, subtle, ancient order, we may be restored to wholeness. A sense of communion with other organisms, with the energies and patterns of nature, is instinctive in children, and it is available to every adult who has ever watched a bird or a cloud. A sense of solidarity not only with all things presently alive, but with generations past and to come, may free us from the confines of the private ego.

18. Recognizing that the land is a unified whole, and that human communities are inseparable from this unity, conservationists must work across the full spectrum of habitats, from inner city to wilderness. And we must engage every segment of the population in caring for our shared home, especially those people who, by reason of poverty or the circumstances of their upbringing, have not viewed conservation as a pressing concern. In other words, conservation must be thoroughly democratic.

19. Our present economy is driven by the pursuit of private advantage. The global market sums up billions of decisions made by individuals and businesses in their own self-interest, with little regard for the common good or for ecological consequences. Therefore, we cannot expect the marketplace to protect the quality of air and water, the welfare of communities, or the survival of species, including our own.

20. As a result of the triumph of the market, the human economy is disrupting the great economy of nature. The same corporations and individuals that profit from this disruption also perpetuate it, by controlling advertising, the news and entertainment media, and much of the political system.

21. Governments and businesses promote endless growth in consumption, which is a recipe for disaster on a crowded planet. Even the slowest growth, if it continues long enough, will exhaust Earth's resources. There is no such thing as "sustainable growth." There is only sustainable *use*.

22. In order to live, we must use the Earth—but we should not use it up. For the sake of our descendants, we must learn to grow food without depleting the soil, fish without exhausting the seas, draw energy from sunlight and wind and tides. We must conserve the minerals we mine and the products

we manufacture, recycling them as thoroughly as a forest recycles twigs, leaves, fur, and bone.

23. Only by caring for particular places, in every watershed, can we take care of the planet. Every place needs people who will dig in, keep watch, explore the terrain, learn the animals and plants, and take responsibility for the welfare of their home ground. No matter what the legal protections on paper, no land can be safe from harm without people committed to care for it, year after year, generation after generation. All conservation, therefore, must aim at fostering an ethic of stewardship.

24. Many of the places we care for will be public—state and national forests, wildlife refuges, wilderness areas, parks. We hold these riches in common, as citizens, and we need to defend them against those who seek to plunder our public lands for the benefit of a few. In an era obsessed with private wealth, private rights, and private property, we need to reclaim a sense of our commonwealth—the realm of shared gifts, resources, and skills.

25. Our commonwealth includes the basic necessities of life, such as clean water. It also includes the basic grammar of life, the evolutionary information embodied in the human genome and in the genes of other species. We should modify that genetic inheritance only with the greatest care, after public deliberation, and never merely for the sake of financial profit or scientific curiosity. We should respect the genetic integrity of other species. We should guard the human genome against tampering and commercialization. These essentials of life belong to all people, and our rights in them need to be fully and forever protected.

26. Even as we defend our public lands, we must encourage good conservation practice on private lands—farms, ranches, fam-

ily forests, factory grounds, city lots, yards. How well these places are cared for will depend on the owners' vision and skill. While conservationists respect private property, we never forget that such property derives its protection from a framework of law, and derives its market value largely from what surrounds it. The public therefore has a legitimate interest in the condition and treatment of *all* land, including that held in private hands.

27. In the long term, we cannot protect land, either public or private, without reducing the demands we make on the Earth. This means examining every aspect of our lives, from our houses and malls to the cars we drive and the food we eat, from our forms of entertainment to our fundamental values, considering in every domain how we might be more thrifty and responsible.

28. While changes in our private lives are essential, they are not sufficient. We must also insure that businesses, universities, foundations, and other institutions practice good stewardship and that governments protect the interests not merely of wealthy elites but of all people, indeed of all creatures. And we must resist the cult of violence that turns homes, workplaces, cities, and entire countries into battlefields. We must therefore engage in politics, supporting candidates and policies that are favorable to conservation and social justice and peace, opposing those that are indifferent or hostile to such causes, making our voices heard in the legislature and the marketplace.

29. If we are to succeed in reversing the current devastation, the attitudes and practices of conservation must become second nature to us, like comforting a hurt child, like planting seeds in the spring. So the aim of conservation must be more than protecting certain parcels of land, vital as that

work is. The aim must be to create a culture informed by ecological understanding and compassion at all levels of society—in the minds and practices of individuals, in households, neighborhoods, factories, schools, urban planning offices, architectural and engineering firms, corporate board rooms, courthouses, legislatures, and the media.

30. In seeking a way of life that is durable, we have much to learn from those indigenous peoples who have lived in place for many generations without degrading their home. When such people are uprooted by enslavement, economic hardships, or war, they are torn away from the ground where their stories make sense. We must help them stay on their native ground, help them preserve their languages and skills, for their experience can enrich our common fund of knowledge about living wisely on Earth.

31. We cannot all be native to the places where we live, yet we can all aspire to become true inhabitants. Becoming an inhabitant means paying close attention to one's home ground, learning its ways and its needs, and taking responsibility for its welfare.

32. Conservationists also have much to learn from people who still draw sustenance from the land—hunting, fishing, farming, ranching, gardening, logging. The most thoughtful of these people use the land respectfully, for they understand that the Earth is the ultimate source of wealth.

33. If we are to foster a culture of conservation, we will need to draw on the wisdom and moral passion of religious communities. Until the past half-century, no religious tradition has had to confront the prospect of global devastation brought on by human actions, yet every tradition offers us guidance in honoring the creation. The world's religions call us away

from a life of frenzied motion and consumption, teaching us to seek spiritual rather than material riches. They remind us to live with gratitude, respect, affection, and restraint.

34. If we are to foster a culture of conservation, we will also need to draw on the full spectrum of science, from astronomy to zoology. We need to know everything science can teach us about how natural systems function, and how damaged systems may be restored. We need to emulate scientists in working cooperatively across nationalities and generations, in adding to the common store of knowledge, in seeking the truth and speaking clearly.

35. Scientists, in turn, need to be guided in their research not merely by what is financially or professionally rewarding, but by what is ecologically and ethically sound—refraining, for example, from research that would turn our genetic inheritance into private property. Whether scientists or not, we should all be concerned with how science is conducted and how technology is applied, for we must all live with the results.

36. While there is much in the work of conservation that we can count—acres saved, whooping cranes hatched, oak trees planted—there is much that cannot be measured in numbers. To convey the full impact of conservation, we need to tell stories, make photographs and paintings, share dances and songs. We need to listen to the people whose lives have been enlarged by a community garden, by the glimpse of sandhill cranes flying overhead, by the spectacle of salmon returning to spawn in a free-flowing stream.

37. Every conservation project tells a story about our values, about our reasons for conserving land or buildings or skills. We should convey these stories as eloquently as we know

how, in words and pictures, in ceremony and song. We draw strength from tales of good work already carried out, from the prospects for restoring landscapes and communities, from the human capacity for taking care, and from the healing energies in the universe.

38. Our largest stories are those of cosmology. Whatever tales we tell about the origin and flow of the universe, and about our place in the scheme of things, will shape our sense of how we should behave. If we imagine ourselves to be participants in a grand evolutionary story, recipients and bearers of cosmic gifts, we are more likely to feel the courage, reverence, and delight necessary for doing good work in conservation over the long haul.

39. Although conservation requires a long-term commitment and a large-scale vision, the work itself is local and intimate, rooting us in our own place, awakening us to our own time, moment by moment. It is joyful work, however hard it may be. In the face of loss, it is brave and hopeful work.

40. Conservation arises from the perennial human desire to dwell in harmony with our neighbors—those that creep and fly, those that swim and soar, those that sway on roots, as well as those that walk about on two legs. We seek to make a good and lasting home. We strive for a way of life that our descendants will look back on with gratitude, a way of life that is worthy of our magnificent planet.

AUTHOR'S NOTE: "A Conservationist's Manifesto" began in lively talk with members of the Center for Land and People advisory board. Scott Sanders wishes to thank his colleagues on the board, including William Cronon, Michael Dorsey, Dianne

Dumanoski, Torri Estrada, Jan Flora, Peter Forbes, Eric Freyfogle, Kurt Hoelting, Mary Evelyn Tucker, Mark Walters, and Alvin Warren. He also wishes to thank Carl Anthony from the Ford Foundation; Michel Gelobter from Redefining Progress; David Grant from the Geraldine R. Dodge Foundation; Kathleen Dean Moore from Oregon State University; and Ernest Cook, Page Knudsen Cowles, Will Rogers, and Kate Williams from the Trust for Public Land, all of whom participated in a January, 2003, meeting at the Wingspread Conference Center in Wisconsin, where he began making notes for the essay. Sanders is especially grateful to Peter Forbes, Eric Freyfogle, Bill McKibben, Kathleen Dean Moore, Ruth McClure Sanders, and Helen Whybrow for reading earlier drafts of the essay and for suggesting how it might be improved. Although "A Conservationist's Manifesto" reflects the insights of many people, it remains a personal statement, one man's attempt to answer the question: How should we live?

SCOTT RUSSELL SANDERS is Distinguished Professor of English at Indiana University. He has published seventeen books, including children's books, novels, and essay collections, notable among which are *Staying Put, Writing from the Center,* and *Hunting for Hope.*

LIFTING THE VEIL

Peter Forbes

Part One: Our Celebration of Life

> If anyone should come upon this capsule before the year
> A.D. 6949 let him not wantonly destroy it, for to do so
> would be to deprive the people of that era of the legacy
> here left them. Cherish it therefore in a safe place.
>
> —message written on the exterior
> of the 1938 time capsule

ON SEPTEMBER 23, 1938, as the sun reached directly overhead, five thousand people who had gathered at Flushing
Meadow fell into silence. It was the autumnal equinox and the
day was unusually clear and cold. They stood on bleachers fac-
ing scaffolding that was positioned over a hole dug in the
ground. At exactly noon, an ancient Chinese bell was sounded
in the background and the scaffolding's steel cables began to
pop and groan as a rocket-like, shining cylinder was solemnly
lowered fifty feet below the ground.

Within the cylinder, engineers had placed a Pyrex tube,
which was first pumped free of air and then filled with nitrogen
gas. Into this tube went a lady's hat, a safety pin, a copy of the
U.S. Constitution, newspapers, magazines, a copy of the Holy
Bible and hundreds of documents of literature and historical
records stored on reels of microfilm. Also included was a guide
for future civilizations (who, it was assumed, would have
moved beyond the English language) to be used in reconstruct-

ing our 1938 American speech and communications. Finally, the cylinder contained letters from leading men of the time: Noble Prize–winning physicist Robert A. Millikan, German novelist Thomas Mann, and theoretical physicist Albert Einstein.

The 1938 time "capsule" was the creation of the Westinghouse Company, a corporation that personified America's unharnessed love affair with technology and commerce and that continues to shape the culture being memorialized in the 1938 time capsule. George Westinghouse, born in 1846, was an inventor who created more than sixty companies and was responsible for the development of alternating current, or AC electricity. Westinghouse Company was chartered when George was forty, founded on his innovative notion that a transformer could supply lighting over a wide area. Four years later, the Westinghouse Company had installed over 300 central power stations. Westinghouse Company, which is now owned by British Nuclear Fuels, aspires to be the leading global nuclear company. Half of all of the world's nuclear power plants today are based upon Westinghouse technology.

The best technology 1938 had to offer was used in creating the capsule, which consisted of 99.4 percent copper, .5 percent chromium, and .1 percent silver. Likewise, the engineers specified exact physical dimensions: seven feet, six inches in length, eight and three-eighths inches in diameter. The cylinder very closely resembled a rocket, and more than one journalist of the day referred to this new creation as a "time bomb" rather than a "time capsule," a name that later stuck.

"Time bomb" is an interesting explanation for what the men and women of Westinghouse had created in 1938; bombs, of course, were on their minds. Stories of that day—September 23, 1938—suggest that Albert Einstein had arrived secretly from Europe early in the morning and was taken by car to Flushing

Meadow were he placed a private letter into the capsule moments before it was sealed. Though no one knows for sure the contents of Einstein's letter, it's very likely that he used it to express privately the same concerns he would express publicly nine months later when he wrote to President Roosevelt, warning that Nazi Germany was building an Atomic Bomb.

Time capsules are, of course, nothing more than mirrors of their creators. What the capsule looks like and where it is deposited are as revealing as what is placed inside. Just these leaders' intention to create the time capsule makes apparent their strong belief in their own achievements and moment in history. But the 1938 capsule is particularly interesting because it exposes so clearly how Americans seemed to consider themselves in relation to the world, including the far future world. It spoke volumes about our sense of invincibility and narcissism. And also our painful naiveté.

Like a poodle burying a bone in the ground, these leaders sank their time capsule fifty feet below the surface of the earth in order to protect it for future generations. But the two atomic fission bombs that America dropped on Japan in 1945, only seven years later, exploded craters 100 feet down and 800 feet across. These leaders were apparently also unaware that natural changes in the earth's axis and continental drift would change the location of the capsule by hundreds of feet during its internment. They went to great lengths to record the precise coordinates of the capsule's 1938 location—40° 44' 34".089 North Latitude, 73° 50' 43".842 West Longitude—in the *Book of Record*, printed on permanent paper with special ink and reproduced in 3,000 copies that were sent to libraries, museums and monasteries throughout the world. Copies were sent to Shinto Shrines in Japan where a powerful military regime was swiftly planning the conquest of the rest of Asia. The *Book of Record* also made its way to India where religious unrest was overshadowed only by protests of colonial rule. And in North America the *Book of Record* was sent across the nation, from the Library of Congress to small libraries in farming towns of Nebraska and North Dakota and others along the shores of New England.

On that autumn day in 1938 the "Capsule of Cupaloy" began its journey five thousand years into the future—not to be disturbed until the year 6949. With this time capsule, its creators hoped "that we might leave records of our own day for five thousand years hence; to a day when the peoples of the world will think of us standing at history's midpoint." They made it a massive, noble, solemn gesture that captured the imagination of the country in 1938, and which now, with the perspective of history, strikes us as freakishly absurd.

To the people who might find this capsule centuries or even thousands of years hence, they inscribed on its side, "let him not wantonly destroy it, for to do so would be to deprive the people of that era of the legacy here left them. Cherish (the capsule) therefore in a safe place." These words, and the act of burying the capsule fifty feet under the ground, accurately reflect the fear and uncertainty that our leaders felt underneath their own bravado. Nothing could create a safe place in 1938, short of a totally different way of living and being in relation with the world, and they must have known this deep inside themselves.

The creators of the time capsule believed that 1938 was a momentous era worthy of positive record. Surely this must be true of every age that seeks to create a history of itself. But on this occasion, history has shown us that 1938 was the threshold of a horrible story. 1938 was the last year that we had the right to call something "unbelievable." In their most violent display of anti-Semitism yet, German Nazis attacked Jewish people and property in Kristallnacht. Hitler annexed Austria. Mexico nationalized its petroleum industries. British Prime Minister Neville Chamberlain and French leaders made the historic "mistake" of appeasing Germany at Munich. Here in America, Woody Guthrie took his one-man, pro-labor folk music show on the road while most Americans were transfixed, instead, by *Snow White and the Seven Dwarfs,* Walt Disney's first full-length animated film.

Perhaps there is a fair connection between the 1938 time capsule and Snow White and the Seven Dwarfs; both offered cartoon-like, peaceful, happy visions of the world. Perhaps that capsule is better described as a time "balm" than a time bomb, in that we used it to make us feel better about or deny what we were doing to the world around us. Even the objects chosen to be included in this time capsule—the lady's hat, the Holy Bible, the reels of microfilm—seem woefully inadequate representations of American culture. The time capsule was the creation of leaders that some have called "our greatest generation," but what was left out was the evidence of the destructiveness and violence of this generation. Not only Walt Disney but also Edward Teller, the inventor of the hydrogen bomb, represented this era. Teller believed that, "we would be unfaithful to the tradition of western civilization if we shied away from exploring what man can accomplish, if we fail to increase man's control over nature." The last sixty-five years have brought about more human death and species extinction than any other time since the ice age. Time capsules are mirrors, direct evidence of our illusions about ourselves, the evidence of our blindness. Sixty-five years later, what are we still blind about? How might we continue to be deluding and diminishing ourselves?

The second millennium inspired renewed efforts at creating time capsules. The *New York Times* launched the most ambitious effort yet, which can be seen, theoretically, for the next 1,000 years above the ground in front of the American Museum of Natural History. The capsule, a 5' x 5' x 5' sculpture of welded stainless steel, was designed by renowned Spanish architect Santiago Calatrava, whose entry was chosen for its startling beauty. It is hopeful that beauty, not a burial underground, might be what will preserve this capsule for the next one thousand years.

Many of the fifty design entrees for the Millennium Capsule were brilliantly inventive, like Jargon Lanier's proposal to load our millennial data onto the DNA of a truly long-lived species, the cockroach, and then simply to allow the cockroach to do what it has already done remarkably well for millions of years: thrive. Maya Lin, architect of the Vietnam memorial, conceived a plan of a metaphor of trees representing the bridge between heaven and earth. She suggested ten English Ivy trees planted at ritual intervals from the capsule, which would be buried deep below Central Park. The pattern of planting would be a proportional spiral used in classical architecture that is found throughout nature—in leaves and trees, the human body and the spirals in sunflowers and seashells, known as the Golden Section. Even after the trees died, their spiral root patterns would remain and lead to the capsule.

The New York Times capsule, which set out to "chronicle life in the late 20th century," was two years in the making and solicited the suggestions and the expertise of many thousands of Americans. When the capsule was sealed on April 26, 2001 it included hundreds of objects, books and records, among them:

> Anti-shoplifting "Gator tag" from Wal-Mart; barbed wire; firearms registration form; advertisement for a Ford Expedition sport utility vehicle; Motorola cellular phone, battery, and brochure; Protector Plus condoms

from Bulawayo, Zimbabwe; Vial of penicillin from
Mantes-la-Jolie, France; Section 17 of the Indian
Constitution from Bharatpur, India; Nickel LP record
containing sounds of the late twentieth century;
David Letterman top ten list; wild apple seeds from
Kazakhstan; perception of tones: pitch and loudness
scales; a copy of the *National Enquirer,* the Holy Bible
in multiple translations; 27 hair samples; Martin
Luther King, Jr.'s "I Have a Dream" speech; Alcoholics
Anonymous book and pamphlets; Internal Revenue
Service Federal Income Tax Form 1040 (2000).

At the installation and dedication of the capsule, Jack
Rosenthal, then editor of the *New York Times Magazine* said,
"Think of the signals we'd be sending if we had gathered today
to bury a barrel: concealment, pessimism, fear of the future,
death. Now think of the signals that this capsule sends to the
next 40 generations: openness, optimism, confidence and trust.
That, finally, is why today is so satisfying. With this capsule, we
declare our faith in the future. With this work of art, we send
forward our celebration of life."

We send forward our celebration of life. These are indeed
meaningful and optimistic words, ideas worth living for. But
are they true reflections of our generation? Have we overcome
the fear and uncertainty of 1938? Are we living a different
relationship with the world around us? Even the most cursory
look at our times suggests a world that remains at war with
itself and with all of life. In fairness to the *New York Times,*
they faced this truth directly with two honest articles that
appeared in the *New York Times Magazine* and which were
also sealed in the time capsule itself. Jared Diamond wrote
about who, in terms of humans, might still be around in the
year 3000:

Nuclear conflict, for all its horror, might not kill every-body. Still, bombs or fallout might destroy every big city on every continent. The only targets that no one will bother to bomb are remote oceanic islands. Their populations will most likely survive, but they will face a problem: almost all of those remote islands are formed of volcanic lava or coral; they are completely without metal deposits. Perhaps there will be enough salvageable scrap metal, but if not, the island popula-tions could, imaginably, relapse into the Stone Age. Only New Zealand has metal deposits and is suffi-ciently large and populous to retain books and knowl-edge of metal technology. Whoever those post nuclear New Zealanders are, it is they who in this scenario would eventually visit the bombed-out and lifeless continents, poke around in the ruins and discover and open the Times Capsule...

There is another type of holocaust, even more likely to halt business as usual. Already, today, we live amid an accelerating environmental calamity as we destroy the world's remaining natural forests, wetlands and fisheries, pollute its air, soil and water and approach the limits of our planet's photosynthetic capacity. It already seems likely that all the accessible supplies of fresh water will before long bump up against the needs of the growing world population — even if that growth rate continues to slow ...

One possible outcome will be familiar to readers of "Riddley Walker," Russell Hoban's chilling depiction of a postnuclear England, bombed back if not to the Stone Age then to no more than the leather-and-wood age. Anyone who has seen a "Road Warrior" movie has a graphic feel for such a primitive society. And that might be the best of it. With only salvage metal on hand, much of humanity would be reduced to the state of hunter-gatherers.

Included in the time capsule was also an article titled, "A Field Guide to the Sixth Extinction" written by Niles Eldridge, a paleontologist and curator at the American Museum of Natural History, which began:

> Species are built to last. The rich fossil record of marine life over the past half-billion years tells us that the likes of clams, corals and crabs typically endure well over five million years. On land, where environmental change more readily upsets the ecological apple cart, the life expectancies of mammals are shorter (though still impressive, on the order of one million to two million years). And yet, here we are at the brink of the year 2000, asking an unnerving question: what species on earth right now will not be here when people open the Times Capsule in the year 3000? . . .
>
> Yet the sad fact is that we are living amid a sixth extinction event—one that, according to the Harvard biologist E.O. Wilson, is costing the earth some 30,000 species a year. Biologists estimate that there are at least 10 million species on earth right now. At this rate, the vast majority of the species on earth today will be gone by the next millennium. Ever since humans domesticated plant crops and barnyard animals beginning some 10,000 years ago, our numbers have shot up from an estimated six million to six billion. We have engaged in a radical, systematic transformation of the world's ecosystems—replacing

grasslands and woodlands with arable fields, cities, suburbs, malls and roadways. We have exploited dwindling stands of timber and fisheries; we have fouled the earth, the atmosphere and even much of the oceans; and we have introduced alien species around the globe. In short, we bear an uncanny resemblance to those Cretaceous comets. . . .

We need the wild congeners of our increasingly homogeneous domestic crops to replenish their genetic diversity. But beyond such practical matters lies a moral question: how can we condone, however passively, the destruction of our fellow species?

What will be long dead when the times capsule is opened in 3000 according to Eldridge? Tigers, many songbirds, pollock, prairie dogs, mahogany, truffles, the African black rhinoceros, the African wild dogs, the Hawaiian coot, the Galapagos penguin, honeybees, the musk ox, *among millions and millions of other species of life.*

How do we make sense of our desire to *send forward our celebration of life* when we are contributing directly to the death of some 30,000 species of life per year?

What do we make of this urge, as reflected by time capsules, to preserve a part of ourselves when we are so clearly destroying the world around us? Time capsules can be valuable and enlivening when they honestly challenge us with questions about ourselves. What do we have today that truly endures? What do we want the people of the future to look back and say about us? What might we give to future generations that is real, alive, true? What are we doing today that represents the full possibility of the human spirit?

I struggle with time capsules because they do not discern between fact and fiction, between what we say and what we do, between our real lives on this earth and the lies we allow ourselves to tell. Time capsules strike me as a human disconnect: that in 2001 we could celebrate the enormous diversity in our culture by placing examples of it into a steel box that will last 1,000 years while simultaneously presiding over the greatest die-off of life in 65 million years. We somehow believe that these artifacts, found by a future generation wholly diminished by the legacy of the past, would say anything other than "damn them." Ultimately, time capsules are about objects as opposed to relationships, and therefore they reinforce the illusion of separation between us and the rest of life. This is an increasingly dangerous notion, one that will certainly kill us. That we can save ourselves while destroying the rest of life is as absurd and immoral as believing that any group of humans could or should create a master race by committing genocide.

Let's take the noble inspiration behind time capsules to ask ourselves how might we truly send forward our celebration of life? How might we create a world, to quote the 1938 time capsule, that the future might cherish? How might we create a time capsule not about objects but about relationships? There are answers in what Rabbi Malka Drucker has written about her people's relationship with Torah:

> For three thousand years, Jews have kept their sacred text, Torah. If we'd stopped with the mere preservation of our oral tradition by putting it in writing, it's not likely we'd still be able to read it. What saved us was not the physical evidence of our civilization, but the constant reading and wrestling with the text to find ourselves within it. We became the holders, the containers of the written text. We became the time capsules for culture, ideas, and dreams of our family.
> We've learned that not even bedrock will preserve

anything forever. We call God *ha tzur,* the rock, because God is the ultimate bedrock, and that immortal substance can only be carried within our physically frail and temporary bodies, yet the word of God, our stone, is what will last forever as long as we keep speaking it. The most precious part of our lives can never be touched. We can touch our noses, but we cannot touch our love, our sense of what is beyond ourselves. Yet we know it, feel it, and through Torah we've learned a way to speak to our children 1000 years from now.

Torah is cryptic, problematic historically, not always great literature, and not always moral. Yet it lives and teaches how to live, because it births our deepest questions and dreams in its very mystery. Let our legacy to the world be a new kind of time capsule, one that is neither buried nor physical, yet one that will last at least another 1000 years. Let us show a new way to preserve the past and at the same time speak to new generations of a new day, a day without war and injustice.

The survival of a scroll is not our triumph. Rather, it's our study of it, our belief in its vision of a perfected world one day, and our faith in Torah's power to purify and enlighten us. Generations of time capsules have given us a document that has empowered us to be like God, active creators in repairing the world.

We can create a new kind of time capsule, not a container for our vanities, but an authentic source of inspiration for how we might better live. This time capsule would challenge our perception of ourselves by being a mirror of our daily relationships with the life around us. Because it lives with us, this time capsule would demand that we grapple every day with its meaning. Most importantly, this time capsule would not be judged by the fabulous and interesting creations we put into it, but by the quality of our relationship to it: by our respect and kinship. We would not place objects of our creation into this time capsule but place, instead, our acceptance of its mystery and our expressions of faith.

Let us think today of how we inhabit the land as the most important time capsule that we might ever create. It shows that we are more concerned about the living heritage we leave for future generations than about any image of ourselves. What we write on the land is a more enduring and accurate reflection of who we are than the artifacts we display. This time capsule says that what we choose to do with the tools we invent is more important than the tools themselves.

Every year I make a pilgrimage to a time capsule. I hike as deep as I can into the red rock canyons of the Cedar Mesa to welcome spring, to hear silence, to briefly escape the mud season of my native New England, and—most importantly—to see one thing. There's a particular natural arch that I always have in mind. At its base can still be seen the evidence of five hundred years of human life: pottery shards, the hollowing in the rock where corn was ground, and the handprints. They always startle me. Hands smaller than my own, still precise with white paint on red rock saying, "I am alive. I have lived."

Perhaps these beautifully subtle explanations of ancient pueblo life are really no different than the woman's hat included in the 1938 capsule or the samples of hair that were taken for the 2001 capsule. All three certainly speak of our determination to express a record of our lives, but what the Puebloans left us, simply left there in nature exposed to hundreds of years of sun, wind and rain, seems so much more enduring, so much more evocative of what I aspire to for myself. The handprints go directly through my rational mind into an ancient memory space that is still connected to the greater world, that knows no distinction between the outline of the human form and the red rock of the canyon itself. It speaks to the part of me that recognizes my own breath in the constellations of Orion. I stare at the handprints because they reconnect me with my own highest aspirations for living: to be in relation to the world around me. The handprints are powerful because they are there, on the rock, still expressing whatever human emotion created them: awe, laughter, fear, anger. One cannot observe them without also smelling sage and earth, without hearing the soliloquy of the canyon wren. I think of the hundreds of generations of deer and mountain lion, and of the hundreds of humans, who, passing through this canyon, have seen these handprints, and moved on. While they are just pigment etched on sandstone, it is their relationship with that place that gives them life. I, too, am nothing more than water and minerals. It is only through my relationships that I transform that water and minerals into a story. And I aspire for that story to be grounded in truth, compassion and a level of awareness of what is going on around me.

I have faith that most Americans recognize that their *true* wealth or security *isn't* in their bank accounts, but comes from the stories we can tell about the people, creatures, and places that we rely upon. Our prosperity and security as people and as members of the natural world can *only* be determined by the quality of our relationships with the world around us, the degree to which we are embedded in the ecological community. This is true for every species of life on this planet. The only honest and truly enduring time capsule is how we live each day in relation to other life, not what we store in a box or accumulate in a bank account.

I also have faith that even as we have witnessed the death of humans, the death of places, and the death of other species, and despite the many lies we have told ourselves about how and why these deaths occurred, we still have the capacity to envision and enact another way of living. Each day, we have the chance to live differently.

Our relationships to land, whether it be a garden on a city block, the knowledge of where our food comes from, or the deep wildness found in a range of forests, rivers and mountains, is the only enduring human story: it is the only story that we can tell about ourselves, now or long into the future, that will be understood and valued. It is the only authentic time capsule for our children's children. And every day it raises important questions of mythic proportions. *How do we want to be?* Do we surrender fully to a culture defined by our own gratification, our own self-preservation and our own death by alienation? Or, do we define ourselves by our tolerance, our sense of self-restraint, and our determination to love and to be loved?

Our most noble and profound time capsule is the daily act of struggling to re-assert our healthy human relationship with the rest of life, to create a new attitude, vision and reality for ourselves. This is the restoration of our lives into the larger story of life.

Part Two: Evolution and Domestication

ALL THROUGH THE morning, we had carefully observed each exhibit, slowly making our way through dark halls of lost people and creatures. Karma Tashi seemed transfixed by each diorama, quietly commenting on the beauty and artistry of the painted backdrops and the realistic eyes of the people and animals. To him this was art, not the story of a diminished natural world. But the exhibits came unrelentingly, one after the other, and the real story of what this museum was telling us became evident. He quietly concluded, "but all the animals are dead."

It was a simple and obvious truth that I had not been able to accept myself with equal frankness. I knew then that I especially didn't want Karma Tashi to see what was somewhere ahead, an exhibit of proud and richly adorned Tibetan people set against some exquisite backdrop of mountains and monasteries. The man and woman would be standing next to one another, each wearing colorful wool jackets, yak leather boots, and necklaces of ancient turquoise. I had been with people just like this, with Karma Tashi's people, except that they were alive and very much in their own living world. They laughed and cried, got married and bore children, worked through the seasons, and slept under the moon. They lived and breathed to tell their stories. I didn't want Karma Tashi to see his own people behind glass. I didn't want to hear him conclude, "but all the people are gone too," and begin to understand the nature of his own extinction. But here we were and my friend walked to the very edge of the display glass and stared for a long moment at the wax figures representing his own people.

As a child, thirty years earlier, Karma Tashi had fled in the middle of winter on foot across the mountains of Tibet. He was following the exodus of the Dalai Lama to live exiled in the Kingdom of Nepal. Now he had flown 12,000 miles to spend the summer in America. He had never before been inside a plane or ridden on a train or seen a skyscraper or touched the waters of an ocean. He didn't know electric lights or television or movies or computers. We walked beside him through this new world, down the streets of New York City, and into the American Museum of Natural History.

Wandering through the exhibits of the world's different peoples with Karma Tashi often felt more like walking through a hardware store than a museum. What seemed like interesting artifacts to me were alive and real to him. He explained how things worked. If it weren't for the glass, he would certainly have picked up the tools, lifted the bowls to his nose to tell him what these different people ate. The beadwork of the Dogon people of West Africa reminded him of things his grandmother had made. The body painting of the Xavante of Brazil reminded Karma of how his people prepared themselves for some Buddhist ceremonies. He stood transfixed by the handprints of both the Aborigines and the ancient Puebloans. The dramatic facemasks of the Wodabe of West Africa reminded him of a Tibetan shaman. He loved the feathered headdresses of the Huichol and told us how they reminded him of his own people's sky burials. We spoke in the present tense about ways of life that were preciously rare or long gone.

And when Karma Tashi came to the Navajo, he paused for a long time and pointed out the turquoise jewelry and the silver hair and the deeply lined faces and saw himself, and in his recognition implied a sense of how these people, 20,000 years ago, had made the journey from Asia across the Bering Strait to North America.

They were like him, but not quite him. He looked upon the Navajo as one of Darwin's famous finches might have looked upon its cousin in the evolutionary journey. But when we came to the display of the Tibetan people dressed in their traditional mountain clothing, it startled me to realize that Karma Tashi was wearing western clothes: khakis, a button-down oxford shirt, and a thin sweater. Karma Tashi was looking more like us than like his own Tibetan people.

Who could blame him for wanting to eat our food, wear our clothes, enjoy what appeared to be our better lives? In coming to America, Karma Tashi believed he was improving his own life and, in a bigger sense, adding positively to the evolutionary journey of his people. Being with him in America, while knowing his history and the story of his people in Nepal and Tibet, made me face painful questions: To what extent is my way of life creating a world of refugees from the land? And what is being gained and lost in this exchange?

That day in the American Museum of Natural History, we spoke for hours about the natural beauty of the clothes and tools we saw. We expressed our awe for the diversity of ceremonies and skills. We marveled at how the people of the Northwest with their totems are so different from the people of the Southeast with their open armadas. We compared these ways of life with the people of the Northeast with their longhouses and wigwams. The unique beauty and richness of each people came from their communion with the weather, with the rivers, with the mountains, and with the forests in which they lived. They looked different, spoke different languages, built different houses, and evolved different mythologies, not solely from human artifice but because the world around them offered these different gifts. The heights of their creativity and humanity came from the depths of their communion with where they lived; their humanness emerged out of the way the mountains touched the skies, the way the trees died in the forest, and the different ways that the creatures cried out to them. The people evolved with their place. And the full implication of this long story is inescapable. What has happened to that diversity of life? Why do we all increasingly look the same today? What is shaping us today *if not the land?*

If you're still smiling, you haven't understood the question.

More and more, we are shaped by a closed and artificial world of our own creation. We are told this smaller, shadow world is sufficient, yet we are rarely satisfied by it. In response, many seem to strive for wealth, thinking money will provide longed-for meaning and safety. Today, our sense of humanness comes largely from gazing upon ourselves and upon our own creations. Our most dominant creation is the technology that permeates all aspects of life and has people going faster and faster to the point where bodies and nervous systems have little physical connection to the world around them. The land is out of body, out of mind, out of sight. Is it any surprise that the average American today can recognize over one thousand corporate logos but can't recognize ten plants or animals native to his own region?

This ignorance frees us up to be what our culture most highly esteems: citizens of the marketplace, global consumers of goods and services. The Canadian social critic, David Suzuki, has written "consumerism has taken the place of citizenship as the chief way we contribute to the health of our society." This focus on what we *own* as the definition for who we *are* may have many positive economic results, but it has also helped to create a deeply personal crisis in how we view our potential and purpose as human beings. By accepting the daily advertisements and the "news" that tell us what to fear, what to desire, how to be in the world, we undermine our own bodies and our own potentials.

Consumerism is today's guiding story for much of the United States and, increasingly, much of the world. It's an age-old story of buying what we once earned for free or didn't think we needed in the first place. And in the process of swapping money for the promise of satisfaction, we remove ourselves one more step from what is real and true in the world. We take one more step toward swapping our lives for lifestyles. We all do it. For over a hundred years, the world's leading human psychologists have painted an increasingly clear picture of the impact of consumerism on our human progress, on our search for meaning. Abraham Maslow saw human development in terms of the process of moving from basic needs (food and shelter) to social needs (love and esteem) to the highest needs of "full humanness," a hierarchy that culminates in the ability to find the sacred in the ordinary. Maslow saw our human aspiration for compassion, truth, goodness, justice, and wholeness as true spiritual values, not the exclusive possession of organized churches but the general responsibility of *all* humankind for how to be in the world.

The consumer culture has greatly expanded our list of "wants" and leads us to believe that our highest development as humans means meeting these desires. It wants us to believe that our legitimate hunger for love, belonging, esteem, and recognition can be met through what we purchase and possess as opposed to how we relate with the world around us. By making this argument in over 30,000 advertisements that our children see every year, the culture highjacks our own human development, replacing our legitimate search for meaning with a yearning for what can never satisfy us. We all recognize this personality of craving and desire, but few of us want it to be the vessel that carries our soul and spirit through the world. We want instead to be defined by our sense of compassion and justice and wholeness with the rest of life. Human beings are both matter and spirit, body and soul. The consumer culture focuses on the matter and the body, confusing physical needs with spiritual objectives. We come to think of our identity in terms of short-lived perks we can give ourselves as opposed to the truly personal acts of our enduring human spirit.

How rarely we experience the truly meaningful; the peak experiences of inspired creativity or altruistic ideals that leave us feeling fulfilled and connected to the rest of life. Is it no surprise that rates of clinical depression in America are ten times what they were prior to 1950? For many people, the "modern life" is a condition of alienation, loneliness, and unarticulated rage. We put no trespassing signs on our land and then upon our own souls.

The twentieth-century psychologist and philosopher R.D. Laing wrote, "Our behavior is a function of our experience. We act according to the way we see things. If our experience is destroyed, our behavior will be destructive. If our experience is destroyed, we have lost our own selves."

How and where do we get another story for ourselves? How do we find again that real experience that might restore ourselves? Today, what are the deeds of great men and women?

The story is here in our direct experience of the land. Thankfully, all we need is already at hand if we can only be strong enough, wise enough, to see it under our feet. The deeds of great men and women are the small, daily acts that preserve our human relationship with the rest of life. From cities to suburbs to small towns, people are re-asserting their need to be connected again, to find more fulfillment in their lives, to restore beauty and to take responsibility.

Looking to the land for our health and meaning is not a nostalgic retreat from the insistent realities of our day. In fact, for most of us, there never has been a golden age when our ancestors lived in perfect ecological health. Most of human life over the last ten thousand years has not been a healthy integration with the land. Looking to the land does not mean going backward, as some would insist, but is the act of going forward differently by taking advantage of the best things our culture has to offer and the best things that the earth has to offer. We are seeking to create a thoroughly new relationship with the land that fully reflects our modern lives. It is the act of confronting life and making real choices about what sustains and what diminishes us.

For some, looking to the land might mean planting a vegetable plot on a city lot. For another it will mean supporting an open space bond referendum in her town. For others, it might mean spending more time with their families hiking and camping. And for someone else, looking to the land might be a quiet act of civil disobedience: simply saying "not me" to the culture that wants us to work, to buy, to conform. Looking to the land is going forward to that new future where we know where our food comes from, where we each take responsibility for creating more health in the world, where we re-assert that our character and our joy come from our relationships to the people and creatures around us. Looking to the land, no matter where one lives, is the personal act of returning to the values that the land has always taught: resilience, continuity, reliability, honesty, patience, tolerance, diversity, awe, connectivity, beauty, and love. Living by those values brings us back to the land, no matter where we live. Returning to them is our challenge, from our hearts and our bodies, to what this world would otherwise have us be.

Losing our connections to the land is not an "environmental" issue. It is first and foremost a human issue. We lose not just our respect for wild creatures; we lose the very wildness that is inside of us. We untether ourselves from the world of life, and we forget just how small an animal we really are. We sacrifice that part of ourselves that is rooted deeply in humility, fairness, and respect. Theologian Thomas Berry writes, "the forest can only become so many board feet of lumber when a certain part of the human mind goes dead. Humans couldn't kill the forest unless there was something already dead in the human intelligence, the human sensitivity, the human emotions. It's a killing of an inner experience."

That inner experience is our wildness. It is our ability to be truly self-willed, allowing the forces of a more-than-human world to shape the highest aspirations for our humanity. It is our ability to lead a unique life driven by our sense of compassion and fairness, our desire to belong, and our knowledge of being part of a story more important than ourselves. Our wildness is our ability to make moral decisions in an immoral world. Our wildness is our capacity to think and act in terms of relationship, kinship, and equity. Our wildness is our originality, our diversity, and our sensuality.

And our wildness is buried deep within us, buried deep in our language. Going back to our words helps us to see that we all once knew these truths. For example, *to remember* is to "connect physically with a place." *To educate* is "to be present." *To respect* is "to look again." *To seduce* is "to lead away". And *apocalypse* is the act of lifting a veil, to see the world as it truly is.

The extinction of this full range of human experience has led the acclaimed Canadian writer and naturalist, John Livingston, to suggest that human beings have become domesticated "with no sense of ecological or interspecies social place," akin to our cats, our dogs, our cows and sheep.

In many ways, we are increasingly domesticated, featureless, and homogenized. And this happened to us because we first did it to the land. Our growing disconnection from the land means far more than the loss of the beautiful places and ways of life that we are unable or unwilling to carry with us. It means more than the arrogance of our humanism. It is a death by alienation.

Is this evolution or is this extinction?

Julian Huxley wrote, "Man is nothing else than evolution

become conscious of itself." Perhaps so many people struggle with fear, alienation, and depression because we are conscious at some level that we have stopped evolving. The part of our humanity that is most vital—our diversity of experience, our awareness, our sense of purpose and optimism for the future—is closer to extinction than anytime in the history of our species.

Others argue that we can solve our environmental problems through technology, and this may be possible in the short term, but what will solve the alienation and meaninglessness?

We are told we should be optimistic about our ever-growing ability to use science to maintain human prosperity. Bioengineering and nanotechnology are today's evidence of our determination to colonize and put under our will every level of the natural world. We replace natural DNA chains with human-created ones. We replace wild forests with domesticated forests or plantations. We replace wild fish with farm-raised fish. We replace wild animals with domesticated animals. We replace our wild, independent, self-willed selves with lesser, domesticated selves. As we increasingly domesticate wild communities, including ourselves, we create the kind of world our philosophy leads us to believe is right. We see fewer and fewer alternatives.

There is a middle path, a teaching for life that is as old as time and still the freshest antidote for what ails us. What is true for the grizzly bear is no less true for the human. We, too, need a natural habitat. All of life seeks the rest of life; we are tuned for relationship. We need wildness in the world and wildness in ourselves to continue a healthy evolutionary journey. The extinction of human experience is parallel and equal to the extinction of biodiversity. We cannot go it alone. We let the grizzly bear die, and we have killed a part of ourselves. We contribute to the homogenization of Karma Tashi and his people, and we have made ourselves less real, less aware, less stable.

Vandana Shiva, an Indian activist, physicist and philosopher, says:

> It is a struggle to protect the freedom of diverse species to evolve; it is a struggle to protect the freedom of diverse cultures to evolve; it is a struggle to conserve both cultural and biological diversity. It is a struggle against new and old forms of colonization.

The middle path, or the radical center, is our struggle to regain a relationship to the land, and to carry it with us in our modern lives as the lesson for how we might better live. In this light, the work of land conservation takes on a purpose and gravity as important as the greatest achievement of any culture: it becomes the noble effort of saving ourselves along with the life that still surrounds us.

This is the renewed awareness of the critical need for *refugia*, seedbeds of life that survive the modern-day glaciers of destruction to enable life to begin anew. The purpose of land conservation is to create refugia, places where humans can re-learn where and how to be in healthy relationship with the rest of life. Refugia are the places that sustain all life, the places where humans and other species can continue to change and evolve together. Refugia contain land and people together.

Some say this is impossible to do, that people have become too destructive, too numerous, too focused on ourselves. I say we must do it. How are we ever going to curb our population, or restore in people some sense of their responsibility to the earth without a strong connection to the land? How will people know what is sacred and essential to a whole life? How can we possibly preserve biodiversity while simultaneously allowing our own human experience to become extinct? It is our relationship to land, in fact, which gives us our highest hope of survival, because it is our relationship to land that has developed our highest values: our sense of patience, commitment, generosity, and belief in a story that is larger than ourselves.

My friendship with Karma Tashi, my devotion to his people, and my own life work in land conservation comes from a passion for the diversity and wildness in this world. Re-thinking land conservation as the conservation of relationships is the rewilding of people and the land. Rewilding means restoring to both people and the land a sense of wholeness or connection to one another because it is only through our relationships with the rest of life that we find our capacity to be uniquely ourselves or, in other words, to be untamed, self-willed, wild.

It is our radical interconnectedness with life that is the source of our capacity to suffer with our world. Take that away from us, and how do you expect us to act?

What most inspires me, what I know to be most true and worthwhile, are all the efforts to record and protect the beauty, value, realness, and interconnectedness of lives that are led in opposition to this mechanical, diminished world of ours. And what connects all of these efforts, large and small, urban and rural, is a love of the land and our embeddedness in it. This is what defeats the extinction of human experience and our death by alienation. Our love of land is the wildness inside of us, saving us and saving the land.

Part Three: Diminishment and Restoration

I HAVE A photograph of an old oak tree spreading its branches and yellow leaves against a crisp blue sky. A young man sits with his back to the trunk, his head turned down. Another tree, a deeply scarred maple, faces him in the foreground. This tree is wrapped with many dying sunflowers and bits of blue ribbon held tightly against its broken bark by a thin, embroidered cotton belt.

I know what happened here. One afternoon in mid September, an old woman was driving fast and casually on a rural road in Maine that she knew by heart. There may have been fog, or a dog that darted into the road, or heart failure, or the unspoken will to die. No one will ever know for sure. The car and the elder sped fast, uncontrolled, off the road and into the heart of the maple tree. A great human being died.

News of Helen Nearing's death, at the age of 91, spread rapidly across New England. It instantly changed my life, whether I understood this or not. I had seen Helen only two weeks earlier when I stopped by her homestead in Harborside to leave the paperwork on the final details of a plan that she and I had been working on for more than three years, a plan that addressed what would happen to her homestead and life work upon her death. In fact, as if reaching out to me from another time, a note from Helen arrived at my home two days after the crash. Her handwriting said, "It's signed. I'm ready."

But I wasn't ready, and neither was the Trust for Public Land (TPL), which was now suddenly being asked to become the steward of a social movement, not just a piece of land. Challenging questions arose immediately as we tried to fill the void created by Helen's death. I had to answer these questions for our board: Does TPL stand for the same things the Nearings stood for? What is the connection between Helen and Scott Nearing and land conservation?

We knew that they lived peacefully on the land for more than fifty years, but they were also powerfully outspoken critics of capitalism and of conventional American culture. Some of TPL's most loyal donors were the bankers, investors, and business people whom the Nearings forcefully wrote were destroying this country. Did Helen and Scott leave their land and rights to their life work to TPL simply because they wanted it conserved, or because they felt they were placing it in the hands of the right tribe, the right lineage of activism? Or, was this a gift that was meant, somehow, to alter the ideas and practices of land conservation? What might this gift of land and livelihood teach a conservation organization?

Scott and Helen Nearing were fearless and resolute in their challenge to existing ways of life, which they saw as enslaving people. In the Buddhist tradition, one would call Helen and Scott *bodhisattvas*; although you may not like what they had to say to you, it would be valuable for you to hear. They had a compassionate belief in the full potential of every human, once liberated, to lead a good life. And in life and death, Helen and Scott were prolific planters of seeds who gave birth to many things. They fed themselves from their own gardens, creating a captivating story about independence, durability, and skill that no doubt spawned the organic gardening movement in the United States. The Nearings had a big hand, as well, in encouraging the birth of land trusts. They inspired the modern back-to-the-land movement that made it popular for so many people across America to live more closely with the land. Many of the idealistic young people who left cities in the 1970s for farms and villages became the same idealistic middle-aged people who later created the land trusts.

The Nearings may have helped to start two influential branches of the environmental movement—land trusts and organic growing—but they themselves would never have called themselves environmentalists. They were interested in social change: evolving the sets of relationships that make for a healthy and just life. Scott Nearing probably would have called "simple-minded" any effort to reduce a complex system to its component parts.

The Nearings embodied an unusual merger of love of land with a commitment to social and economic justice. So did another man, Aldo Leopold, whom many call the father of the American land ethic. Nearing and Leopold were born at roughly the same time, Leopold in 1887 and Nearing in 1883. Separated by thousands of miles and different backgrounds, they would have been unlikely to meet. But we might contemplate how their ideas and practices overlapped and dovetailed. How can we learn from both of them, and, with their help, move toward a synthesis of a clearer and richer vision?

Leopold grew up in Iowa, took his first job in New Mexico in the newly created U.S. Forest Service, and less than ten years later was chief of operations for the southwest region of the country. He later became a professor at the University of Wisconsin, served as the head of many organizations, and helped to found several enduring ones, such as the Wilderness Society. In each setting, Leopold emerged as an innovator and leader. He was that rare breed of good scientist, passionate human, and skilled communicator, giving us almost 500 published works concerning soil erosion, game management and land philosophy. At the age of forty-eight, Leopold bought a farm on the Wisconsin River which became the setting for his famous natural history sketches, A Sand County Almanac, which fifty years later continues to inspire the practice of land conservation.

Scott Nearing was raised in Pennsylvania and graduated from the Wharton School where he went on to teach as an economist. He earned a national reputation very early in his life for opposing privilege and power and for speaking out against war, child labor, and unequal treatment of women. He was fired from the Wharton School in 1915 for his religious and economic views and, two years later, was dismissed from the University of Toledo for his anti-war activities. A popular teacher and public speaker, Nearing left academia to join the socialist party and to run unsuccessfully for a congressional seat. Undeterred by these losses, Nearing continued his outspoken stance against the war and was indicted and eventually acquitted under the Espionage and Sedition Acts. When Scott was forty-nine, in 1932, Scott and Helen decided to separate themselves from capitalist society and culture to experiment with a new life— what they would call *the good life*—of homesteading, providing for all their own needs through a close, personal association with the land.

Leopold spent forty years studying and writing about the interdependencies of members of the land community, including humans, and how people might relate to the land in healthy ways. Leopold came to understand and emphasize the importance of the interrelatedness of human ethics, science, and the health of people and the land. He dovetailed ecological, scientific evidence with human morality, coming to reveal the need for an ecological attitude toward life: "a land ethic changes the role of *homo sapiens* from conqueror of the land-community to plain member and citizen of it." The growth of his own ethical consciousness may be measured in *A Sand County Almanac*, published posthumously in 1949. Selling poorly at first, by the 1970s it would become a sort of conservationists' bible, eventually outselling even Rachel Carson's *Silent Spring*.

Scott and Helen's most famous statement of their beliefs, *Living the Good Life*, was first published in 1954 and was compared almost immediately with Thoreau's *Walden*, as it offered a twentieth-century account of liberation through an alternative way of life. Scott Nearing wrote, "living the good life for us was practicing harmony with the earth and all that lives on it. It was frugal living, self-subsistent, self-sustaining."

Leopold wrote about the health of land and the Nearings wrote about the social health of our country. Both wrote directly and specifically from a deep, first-hand experience of the land. Today, Leopold is a conservation icon and Nearing remains an iconoclast. Why is that?

Many of their differences, of course, emerge from their backgrounds and personalities and less so from their beliefs. The two men represent important differences in approach that can today inform those of us who seek to care for the land. Both saw the same problem: a decaying and unjust culture increasingly separated from an ailing land. Nearing's early political pursuits pitted him directly against a system that he spent the first half of his adult life trying to change. Eventually, Nearing would choose to live outside that system, and this path of life-as-dissent was deeply inspirational and valuable to a great many people. Leopold probably saw capitalism as a system that wouldn't change and therefore directed his energy toward trying to reform, not replace, the system. Leopold's core belief was in the connection between health and whole systems: "A thing is right only when it tends to preserve the integrity, stability, and beauty of the community, and the community includes the soil, waters, fauna, and flora, as well as people." Nearing believed in the same wholeness of life, but sought it out and defined it more in terms of justice and fairness, as when he wrote in 1946, "This is the ethical and moral lesson of the ages—treat your rival better than he treats you; eschew victory; avoid any suggestion of superiority; understand; sympathize; share. All men are members of great family, in which they must live and help others to live."

Nearing and Leopold strove for a new set of ethics and were strong dissenters from modern society. If there is a difference

in their work, it might be that Leopold went further than
Nearing in defining his core vision in ways that future generations could continue to wrestle with and make contributions
toward. Nearing gave us a new definition for the good life that
many are trying to live by, but Leopold's plea for an Ecological
Conscience linking healthy people and healthy land is more
accessible to larger numbers of people.

Let's imagine for a moment. It's 1948 and Aldo Leopold is waiting to hear whether the set of essays destined to become *A
Sand County Almanac* will get published. Unusually, instead of
heading out to The Shack one April weekend, Leopold decides
instead to travel to Vermont to meet up with his old friend and
fellow founder of the Wilderness Society, Benton MacKaye.
MacKaye takes Aldo to see Stratton Mountain, the place that
inspired MacKaye to dream of the creation of the Appalachian
Trail. And while on Stratton Mountain, MacKaye takes
Leopold over to the small community of Pikes Falls to meet a
well-known couple: political activists, homesteaders, fellow
writers. MacKaye knows that Leopold, who is himself passionate, contemplative and very practical, will like these two and be
inspired by their "experiment in living."

Scott and Helen greet Aldo by handing him a shovel and they
head out to work together. While weeding the large garden and,
later, while repairing a stone wall, they learn about each other's
life work. That evening, a larger collection of men and women
gather at Forest Farm for a simple meal and a long evening of
conversation. Leopold also meets a young man, Richard Gregg,
who had worked in India with Mahatma Gandhi. Gregg gives
Leopold a pamphlet he wrote called "Voluntary Simplicity."
Leopold is moved by these new friends whose political stands
are matched by the choices they have made in how they lead
their daily lives. Their deeds closely match their creed. There's

a seamlessness in their lives that Leopold has also worked hard to establish in his own life. He has devoted much of the last five years to defining what he means by a "land ethic" and here are people living a version of it. Leopold lies awake for much of the evening thinking about his own life in service to the land. For Leopold, this has meant greatly valuing his relationships with his many students and with the citizens with whom he's worked over many years, as well as his ability to influence society's leaders. And he recognizes the enormous importance to his thinking that has come from his own "experiment in living" the last fifteen years at his shack along the Wisconsin River. Though Leopold has always sought to engage society differently than the Nearings, he values their lives and their teachings and is eager to take what he has learned from them. He is also a man who has led group efforts, and his mind shifts naturally to what he can do with the awareness that is swirling in his head. He envisions a new sort of organization, one devoted to the land but that also helps to create a new kind of people. Such an organization, were it to exist, might be based on these principles:

- Our love of the land is inseparable from a strong social conscience. We cannot adequately care for the land without caring for one another, and vice-versa.

- Our love of the land calls upon us to dissent from a society that is destroying it. Our love of the land calls upon us to join together into a common cause, to imagine together an ecological vision, which includes humans as special members of the land community. This must affect what we eat, value and how we live.

- Our love of land begins, first and foremost, at home.

Aldo Leopold never met Scott Nearing. Worse, Leopold died at the age of sixty-one of a heart attack while fighting a grass fire. But we desperately need what we can synthesize from their lifework into a potent, vivid image for today's society.

A few years before his death Leopold wrote, "there are two things that interest me: the relationship of people to each other, and the relationship of people to the land." Had he lived longer to make this unified statement the focus of the last half of his life, today we might have a much different conservation movement. Leopold might have become the leader who gave us the concept of a land ethic *and* helped people to see how they could live by it. It is a strong foundation that views the world as an integrated whole. It binds together the health of the land and the health of the people. It balances the power of our scientific understanding with the wisdom of our emotional intelligence. Taken to its logical conclusions, as Leopold might have done had he lived another twenty years, this foundation allows conservation to become more of a social movement where protecting the earth is an act of giving voice to the voiceless, fostering true democracy, and saving ourselves while saving the land.

Today's conservation movement needs a better synthesis of the different approaches taken by Aldo Leopold and Scott Nearing. Both were deeply committed to the relationships between the soul of the land and the soul of our culture, but their approaches represent different wings of activism—the radical and the reformer—that need to be made whole for the conservation movement to reach its greatest influence. No single approach ever succeeds. Are we any closer than we were in 1949 to a land ethic that is as widely recognized as, say, women's rights?

The conservation movement is plagued by a curse of separation. It has separated people from biodiversity. It has separated, and then confused, its tools with its objectives. It has separated many of its activists from the source of their activism. It has separated *itself* into highly technical organizations: ones that focus on endangered species, or wilderness, or farmland, or urban greening, or historic preservation, or local open space. We've lost, or never had, the big picture, the view that sees the possibility of the world as a unified whole. Worse, we have allowed ourselves to be further separated into the false divisions of radicals and reformers, idealists and dealmakers. Today, to meet the scale of problems that face us, we all need to be reformers with radical hearts. We need the reformation Aldo Leopold offered with the radical ideas of right livelihood expressed by Helen and Scott Nearing. If we could combine the approaches of Leopold and Nearing we would have a serious and complete response to the destructiveness of modern life as well as a full and rich ecological vision for how to better live.

Perhaps it should not surprise us that the same forces that have diminished our land have also diminished the effectiveness of our activism. We've fallen headfirst into the trap of believing that technical solutions—the buying of land or the passing of laws—are adequate solutions for our moral and ethical problems. They are the tools, the means, but not the long-term objectives that we must always keep in mind: pulling down the cultural walls that we have built between ourselves and the rest of life. The big picture solution offered by land conservation is healthy people and healthy land: an integrated, unified view of awe and justice combined.

Our activism is mostly in response to fixing what is broken, as opposed to offering a vision for what might be restored. We are excellent at talking about what needs to be stopped, but very poor at talking about what needs to be started. We are forceful in saying what we are against, but timid in saying what we are for. Our neighbors want to know what they can do to live saner, more joyful and connected lives, while we are struggling to keep the Endangered Species Act intact, to stop encroachments into our wilderness areas, or to defeat transportation initiatives which destroy both our cities and our countryside. We haven't connected the dots. We valiantly and consistently perform these technical solutions and save the day, but are then saddened and disheartened when our neighbors don't understand the meaning of what we've done.

In the course of ten years helping communities to protect the places that matter most to them, I have often heard some version of the statement: "the world I knew is gone." It became a poignant rallying cry for TPL's conservation work and I repeated it from community to community. People recognize loss in their own lives. But confronting diminishment alone isn't the positive statement that makes land conservation truly transformational. Focusing solely on the loss in our lives caters to fear and to unsatisfying hopes of stopping all change, both of which rarely contribute to a positive future. Instead, what do we want to carry forward with us? What matters most?

After talking with a group of conservationists in Austin, Texas, I was approached by a woman who told me that she had grown up in Billerica, Massachusetts, the hometown of one of my favorite stories about land and people: the saving of Griggs Farm. In the mid 1990s, this community made a very difficult and contentious decision to save one of their last working farms to keep it from becoming another big box store. It was the first time they had ever conserved land, and that process of activism enlivened the community after years of being beaten down by land use decisions that felt completely out of their control.

Sheila told me that after the farm was conserved things were different in Billerica. She spoke about the conservation project setting a benchmark for tolerance that is still upheld. The act of conserving land helped them to distinguish between loyalty and citizenship, characteristics that are often confused. Many places are fiercely loyal to their clubs, charities and congregations, fiercely loyal, in other words, to their own kind—the narrowly defined membership that includes people like them. That was changed in Billerica. Citizenship came to mean being open to new people, new ideas, new traditions. They saw many possibilities for themselves. They started thinking about a healthy future not just in terms of economic growth but in terms of relationships. A new group of leaders was elected. Working to save that farm told a new story about Billerica that people were increasingly proud of. It was a story about the value of diversity and the power of restoration, one that showed how the people of Billerica have many vital definitions of their humanity. It said that their values as a community included tolerance, sacrifice, humility, and mutual aid. The act of conservation helped bring people together and made them less fearful of one another. And by speaking and acting in clear terms about what they loved, as opposed to what they feared, their struggle over land enabled them to address other fundamental issues in their lives, such as the quality of their schools and the fairness of their community. In a town where land conservation was unheard of seven years before, newly elected officials adopted stricter land use controls in order to protect what biodiversity remains. In striving to find what was most meaningful and what might contribute most to their sense of belonging to a larger community, the people of Billerica found the path to their own ecological health. Leopold wrote that "ecological conscience is therefore the ethics of community life."

The people of Billerica responded to that farm in a way that changed them and their community forever. It wasn't just stopping a Wal-Mart that made the difference, it was the clear vision for what they could restore to themselves and how they might imagine their lives differently. We all want our lives to tell a rich story, one that expresses what we really love, what inspires us, what matters most.

And this story always raises valuable questions. Do we surrender to a culture defined by self-interest and apathy toward community, or do we choose, instead, to be defined by our self-restraint and a sense of service? To save land is to suggest that humans are not the only measure of things, that humans can be defined more by their fairness and compassion and desire to belong.

These expressions of service, tolerance, and humility are core values that most people want, but that have never been easy to live by. Today it's even harder. But these values left in our hearts by conservation are bigger and more important than we can imagine. They are bigger than we can possibly count in acres. They are bigger, even, than can be expressed in the saving of endangered species. These values given to us by a connection to land are so important that they stand to re-define what it means to be human in this century.

The story of diminishment is an awfully long one, perhaps center stage since the industrial revolution. The Norwegian philosopher Sigmund Kwaloy formulated the term "industrial growth society" to describe a culture increasingly shaped and manipulated by its commercial systems of design and production. The industrial growth society, for example, demands efficiencies in production—the assembly line—that have been transferred over to other facets of life. The way we develop land has become a powerful force in making everywhere look the same, reducing our affections and loyalties to what was once local and unique. The industrial growth society relies on an ever-expanding base of consumers who are ready and willing to take on larger and larger amounts of personal debt, which has helped to separate people from the land by concentrating people in cities where there are more and better paying jobs and by making free time scarcer and scarcer in people's lives. The industrial growth society has fattened our pocketbooks, lengthened our lives, and created more economic opportunity, but it has also created vast inequities and required that most people give up many things that were once held dear. So much of our lives seem to be about having more, but feeling less. The industrial growth society views the diversity of life on earth not as an elegant, complex and life-giving force but, instead, as an obstacle in the effort to go faster and faster.

Certainly, we can do much better, but where do we want to go and how do we get there? This question was the fundamental theme of Aldo Leopold's life work and led him to conclude that we needed one overall goal for conservation, which he called "land health."

If there is ever to be change in culture that might save our species it will need to come out of the pull of love, joy, and restoration of healthy human life rather than the push of fear. No change will come out of any force that is not fundamentally grounded in an ethos of restoration. Restoration, or the reconnection of our lives to the health of the land, is the parable for a healthy human future.

Human love is a vital and yet complicated part of the solution. But what do we hope our love will create? And, while being open to expressing our love, we must recognize that people express love in many different ways, some of which aren't healthy. Love can be liberating and it can be possessive. I value Leopold's bottom line, which is "a thing is right only when it tends to preserve the integrity, stability, and beauty of the community, and the community includes the soil, waters, fauna, and flora, as well as people."

But imagine how difficult this is in a culture dominated by

fear. Fear is everywhere. We fear change. We fear one another. We fear what's being taken away from us. We fear what we can and cannot do. We fear knowing the truth. We fear what might be done to us. We fear truly feeling the beauty and the dis-ease of the world. Our culture plays upon fears, as has been amply demonstrated by the advent of national security warnings in the twenty-first century, which don't tell us what to be afraid of but just that we ought to be afraid. Fear leads to *meaninglessness*.

The environmental historian William Cronon says, "one of the greatest contributions to sprawl has been our fear. White people flee the cities because they fear what will be taken away from them. Our fear of losing something drives us to destroy the very thing we're fearful of losing in the first place." And we've reached the point where all of this loss and fear has become completely normal and accepted as the inevitable cost of doing business. But it is far from normal.

Making *normal* such losses is a form of apocalypse. The activists in India who have been fighting the dam on the Narmada River have a saying that "you can wake someone who is sleeping but you cannot wake someone who is pretending to be asleep."

Apocalypse is about people who are pretending to be asleep. It's an important word that most associate with the final catastrophe or the end of the world. There is, however, a positive, even hopeful meaning, of apocalypse, which is Greek for *revelation, to reveal, or to lift the veil*. Imagine if everyone in America could lift a veil and suddenly see the world with new eyes, as it truly exists. We don't necessarily need more data, more reports, *we need new eyes*. We need to be awake. And we need to be brave enough not to run away from what we see when the veil is lifted so that the era of *restoration and rehabitation* can begin. Today, whether we know it or not, we are choosing which meaning of apocalypse our children will live with: the end of the world or the era when the veil was lifted.

Can we evolve fear of change into a dance of renewal? How do we help everyone to lift the veil? We need more truth-telling followed by resolute action. Lincoln warned us that America could not survive half-slave and half-free, and then he sacrificed his life attempting to rectify the problem. The truth of our era is that we will not survive as a culture or a species if we continue to destroy the rest of life that is here.

Another hard truth is that our conservation movement will never be able to offer a compelling story of hope or positive solutions for our culture, which is increasingly made of haves and have-nots, without first proving that we are fair and equitable in all our ways. We must courageously face the truth that even though all Americans deserve a relationship to the land through healthy food, access to parks, and clean air and water, these benefits of conservation have fallen most often to middle- and upper-class white Americans. Conservation historically has not been fair or equitable, and many Americans who love the land do not love conservationists because of this. We make a critical error in judgment that can be seen clearly by others whenever we fail to recognize that how we treat one another is just as important as how we treat the land.

Is it ever right for one group to have so much when others have so little?

Our awareness of this truth requires neither blame nor guilt, but that our present action emerges from our ability to listen to different voices, to be compassionate and tolerant, and that our conservation seeks a respectful realignment of power. Nothing we protect will be permanent, regardless of what the legal language says, if we don't also create broad-based support and more democratic conservation organizations. There is no short-cut to achieving this integrity, only honest and open steps to take toward it.

Another truth is that we can resolve many of the problems

that we have created. What we need is already at hand, but we must get much better at putting our most ambitious goals in simple terms so that more people can say, "we can do that." Oberlin College professor David Orr reminds us that, "we have always known enough to do better than we are doing now." E.O. Wilson writes in *The Future of Life* that "to save 70 percent of the world's remaining biodiversity would take only one-thousandth of the current annual world domestic product, or roughly $30 billion out of approximately $30 trillion. One key element, the protection and management of the world's existing natural reserves, could be financed by a one-cent-per-cup tax on coffee." Americans are completely capable of marshalling this level of resources. After all, we spent more than $30 billion on waging a five-week war in Iraq. What is our political will for helping to conserve the rest of life on this planet?

My last answer to the question, *how do we help everyone to lift the veil,* is to return to Aldo Leopold and Scott Nearing and explore how they might have asked us to re-think the promise of land conservation.

Scott Nearing saw his love of land and his social conscience as inseparable. In 1965, he wrote: "It is no more possible to separate humanity from its environment than it is to separate trees from the earth in which they grow, or to separate a finger from the hand on which it lives. Man and his environment are two parts of one totality." In 1972, Nearing wrote "each human being feels, thinks, and acts personally, socially and also as a part of nature, as part of the universal whole." Leopold wrote in 1940, "conservation, viewed in its entirety, is the slow and laborious unfolding of a new relationship between people and the land." These are powerfully important thoughts that are too often disregarded by the modern conservation movement, which has paid too much attention to the direct insults to human health or to biodiversity and too little attention to the big picture: to the whole system of healthy functioning land of which people are a part. This separation is what has allowed us to create a science of land protection that aspires to protect endangered species of plants and animals without considering how simultaneously to aid the alienated, addicted, joyless human being.

Stewart Udall wrote: "True conservation begins wherever people are, and with whatever trouble people are in."

Nearing and Leopold would remind us that our love of land calls upon us to dissent from the society that is destroying the land. Nearing's legacy to conservationists is the strength and will to ask ourselves, in the words of Wallace Stegner, is land conservation any more than the effort of a comfortable middle-class to preserve its amenities? Should conservation say something more emphatic about the wrongness of self-interest and the destructiveness of our consumer culture? Nearing was clear on that. In 1914, he wrote "the individual must find salvation from an exacting standard of achievement in a reconstructed philosophy that will make him the master, and not the slave of the things he possesses." And, in 1954, "our Vermont project was a way of preserving self-respect and of demonstrating to the few who are willing to observe, listen and participate, that life in a dying acquisitive culture can be individually and socially purposeful."

It is healthy to consider land conservation as a form of civil disobedience that quietly but steadfastly opposes the prevailing cultural forces of our times. Let's be fully awake to the vision of a united movement working toward the well-being of land and people. Everyday, we can quietly ask ourselves a deeply radical question, how much is enough? Our culture, of course, wants us to believe that we never have enough, but we know differently. A single farm protected against the encroachment of sprawl tells a different story than the story offered on television. That protected forest in the middle of town, for example, tells a story about respect, limits, resilience, durability, local knowledge, geography, beauty, and mystery and *exactly how much is enough.* Thinking of land conservation as quiet civil disobedience and a means toward healthy land and people helps us to envision conservation as a social force. Our determination to protect these special places calls upon us to make sacrifices, to express our ideals and hopes in ways that many of us have never before been asked to do. There is a sense of loss that is felt by far more Americans today than in 1948 when Leopold completed *A Sand County Almanac.* This generation, more than any other, is living with the homogenized, sterile, disoriented, disconnected, rootless culture of our making, and many are saying "enough is enough." Given an alternative to the life at hand, many of us will rise to the challenge of living differently and, in so doing, redefine ourselves as citizens. Conservation is the tangible, highly visible expression of our own *ethics of enough.*

Leopold was nervous about a form of conservation that was valueless, that "defines no right or wrong, assigns no obligation, calls for no sacrifice, implies no change in the philosophy of values." He was concerned that conservation would become only an outlet for human recreation, as opposed to becoming an inspiration for human re-creation. And he was right; land conservation still doesn't talk enough about values. Not often enough does land conservation teach and stretch us to act differently.

Five years before *Sand County Almanac* was published, Aldo Leopold wrote to his friend Doug Wade who was the naturalist at Dartmouth College, "nothing can be done without creating a new kind of people." Later Leopold would write, "conservation is one of the squirmings which foreshadow this act of self-liberation." Let us begin to think of our relationship with land,

then, truly as an act of self-liberation from ways of living that
deny us meaning, connection, and purpose. And let us think of
land conservation as the work of taking us beyond ourselves.

The third idea given to us by the imagined collaboration of
Leopold and Nearing is that conservation begins at home. John
Saltmarsh, Scott Nearing's biographer, wrote that for Nearing
"the home in homesteading signifies nature as a place where
one lives—the wild is close to home—where the well-being of
the natural world and humankind are intertwined." It's an idea
that Thoreau, too, would have appreciated. Henry David
Thoreau penned his now famous line: "In wildness is the
preservation of the world" while living in decidedly suburban
digs. True it was a cabin of less than 100 square feet built at a
cost of only $28.00 but what few remember is that Walden was
no wilderness. When Henry lived there, he could easily hear
five times a day the whistle of the commuter train that passed
within a quarter mile of his cabin. And a good meal and a place
to wash his laundry was less than a mile away in town.

It's important to understand this, to credit Thoreau for writing something about wildness so powerfully symbolic and moving in a place that was hardly wild. The point being that
Thoreau found wildness there in himself, and in the wood-
chuck that ate his beans, and in his deep attachment and love
for the place. His relationship with that pond enabled him to
become more self-willed, or wild.

And it's a good thing, because the man and the book have
made a huge difference. In one of history's great connections,
Gandhi drew inspiration for much of his thinking while in jail
in 1908 reading a story by another jailed dissenter, one Henry
David Thoreau. So, a rather average pond in eastern
Massachusetts inspired at least one man, and that one man
went on to inspire the world. People now flock to Walden Pond
because of the relationship between that man and his pond and

what that relationship led to. The Trust for Public Land and I spent five years working on the effort to protect Walden Pond, and the lesson that is most memorable is this: every community has a Walden Pond, a simple place that can inspire a single individual. It's the relationship between the person and his or her geography that continues to inspire people.

Wallace Stegner wrote about home: "There is only this solid sense of having had or having been or having lived something real and good and satisfying, and the knowledge that having had or been or lived these things I can never lose them again. Home is what you take away with you."

I sat with Helen Nearing a few weeks before her death, knowing nothing of the future, and spoke about what work she felt was left undone in her life. She was especially concerned that the reasons for which she and Scott lived not be lost to enthusiasm for the particular way they lived. Helen wanted, above all, for the political, socio-economic, and spiritual principles that they lived by to endure along with the land itself. And she mentioned a sadness that she and Scott's lifework, which began in the cities, had become associated mostly with rural life. She was moved by my stories that afternoon of urban gardens and the efforts of so many people to re-define themselves by sinking their hands into the earth. And now, years later, we are still grappling with the question of how to knit together the land and ourselves. How do we defeat the illusion of separation? How do we stop the diminishment and begin the era of restoration?

It's a question both Aldo Leopold and the Nearings struggled with. Their lives reflect an attitude that can bear many different expressions all held within the same theme: the health of the people is dependent upon the health of the land.

One summer several years ago, I was at Forest Farm when an old station wagon pulled into the farm with Indiana plates and an overheating radiator. A middle-aged man got out and walked around to the back of the car and, with great effort, took out a very large rock and walked with it fifty feet to the garden wall where he left it. He had traveled a thousand miles to see and walk on the land that had inspired Helen and Scott. Later, after my Indiana friend had left, I saw that he had inscribed a single line on the stone: "Born originals, how come it to pass that so many of us die copies?"

Part Four: Meaningful Resistance

"Born originals, how come it to pass that so many of us
   die copies?"

—Edward Young

WHAT DID THAT stone and its inscription mean?

This line from Edward Young's poetry gradually helped me to understand more deeply why we conserve land. In placing the stone by the garden wall, this man from Indiana helped me to understand what Scott Nearing had to teach us. Re-connecting with the land is to find our own source of meaning and uniqueness, to help us avoid dying copies of one another. Scott's social conscience made it clear that the point of life is not just to free yourself to reach your own dreams, but to live a life that frees others. The purpose of conservation, then, is to preserve the freedom and honor of living within the wholeness of all life. And when we grasp, on a early fall morning, our humble embeddedness in the community of life, we glimpse the full miracle that life has bestowed on all without discrimination. Every step we take that honors the diversity of life elevates our spirit; every step we take that diminishes life diminishes our spirit.

A few thousand people make their way each year to the gardens and stone home built by Helen and Scott Nearing for the same reason that others hike through the Sierra backcountry, because they yearn for experiences that might nurture the potential of their human spirit. These are pilgrimages of communion, where our connection with another way or form of life helps to defeat the diminishment in our own lives and helps us to find what is true and unique inside ourselves. This modern world of ours tolerates these pilgrimages when we are young, when we can throw on a backpack and see the world in order to find ourselves, but what about when we are older, say when we are a middle-aged man from Indiana? No, in our older years, we reward conformity and we disparage dissent. We hardly tolerate the musings of older men and women. We call those who are still seeking new solutions idiosyncratic or curiosities, and we assume that they have lost their bearings. Why does our industrial growth society demand such loyalty and fear such dissent?

In my darkest hours, I recognize how much our industrial growth society demands a world made of copies and I see the degree to which we have complied. Though born an original, my own life has become something of a copy. The brave people who have resisted and who now find themselves on the margins of culture have always had something very important to teach us, and the value of that teaching grows every year. Rudolf Bahro, the German philosopher and political activist, explained that these are the people who can still show us the way. "When the forms of old culture are dying, the new culture is created by a few people who are not afraid to be insecure."

Our lives have been rescued time and time again by those who have felt terribly insecure.

Roughly forty years ago, a revolution began. Some say it started in 1962 with the publication of Rachel Carson's *Silent Spring*, but that was the climactic event of a much longer and more painful evolutionary process. Humanity had already experienced two all encompassing revolutions, both of which were fundamentally about relationships. Ten thousand years ago, the agricultural revolution prompted us to organize ourselves from hunter-gatherers into nation-states. And, roughly two hundred years ago, the industrial revolution greatly accelerated this same change to take us from citizens of nation-states to laborers and consumers of a global capitalism. Each of these revolutions changed the way we viewed ourselves and the world around us. Each of these revolutions contributed important advancements to our quality of life, but each also has had a dark side: each has further separated us from one another and the land and has created a resulting set of pathologies. The psychologist Thom Hartmann explains such human transition as "the breaking of the intimate bond with the world around us, the separating of ourselves into increasingly isolated 'boxes.'" Another psychologist, Theodore Rorzak, put it this way, "the earth hurts, and we hurt with it." In other words, every tear in the earth became a tear in us.

One can view the last ten thousand years of human evolution as the process of burning the bridges to the world around us, the process of creating our own human-made culture at the expense of our relationships with the rest of life.

Rachel Carson drew the world's attention to ways we had divorced ourselves from life. Her articulate, compassionate voice woke us up to the multitude of deaths we were causing. She wrote, "the more I learned about the use of pesticides, the more appalled I became. What I discovered was that everything which meant most to me as a naturalist was being threatened, and that nothing I could do would be more important." On the eve of *Silent Spring's* publication, Carson wrote to her dearest friend Dorothy Freeman, "I know you dread the unpleasantness that will inevitably be associated with its publication ... but knowing what I do, there would be no peace for me if I kept silent."

Rachel Carson opened our eyes to our responsibility for the death that was around us, and she gave voice to our sorrow. It was a palpable grief for the loss of songbirds and the loss of our own family members to new cancers. The response from the industrial growth society was ferocious. She was called a bogus scientist and a "hysterical woman." The attack on the book and on her personally must have been motivated by a deeper anger than merely the loss of profits for the pesticide companies. She was challenging our very way of life. Paul Brooks, Carson's longtime editor, described it this way: "Her attackers must have realized that she was questioning not simply the use of poisons, but the basic irresponsibility of our industrial society toward the natural world: the belief that damage to nature was an inevitable cost of 'progress'. That was her heresy."

She wrote to Dorothy, "The beauty of the world I was trying to save has always been uppermost in my mind—that, and anger at the senseless, brutish things that were being done. I have felt bound by a solemn obligation to do what I could—if I didn't at least try I could never again be happy in nature."

Silent Spring quickly found a huge international audience—twenty-three separate language editions within three years—because it spoke the truth and helped us to bear witness to ourselves. It marked a shift in our worldview by helping us to see clearly that who we are is *not* measured by what we own and control. We can not escape the fact that we do have a conscience, a sense of right and wrong, and a set of moral obligations. Who we are can only be measured, therefore, by our moral actions. Slowly, painfully, we recognized that our prosperity could not possibly grow at the expense of the rest of life. The meaning of who we are comes from our relationships with the world around us, human and non-human. That is the gold; everything else is just cheap and dangerous glitter.

This emerging consciousness (what Leopold called the Ecological Conscience) is the foundation of the *ecological revolution*, or, as systems thinker Joanna Macy puts it, "a time of revolutionary ecology." Or, as E.O. Wilson describes it, "the century of our environment." This is the integration of our sophisticated modern lives into the whole of life. It's the story of how a re-thinking of our relationships can be the path to creating an alternative future to the industrial growth society.

If, one hundred years from now, there are still mountain lions and salmon, piliated woodpeckers and grizzly bear, right whales, honey bees, and places for people to see their own evolutionary potential, then it will be due to land conservation. What we don't proactively save today through forethought, action, and wisdom, chances are won't be here when our children are adults. And as much as conservation is succeeding in creating refugia, or safe havens for pockets of diverse life that might survive the industrial growth society, we conservationists are failing to take the risks necessary to help people live differently, to envision and create an alternative culture. That alternative culture won't emerge solely because land has been protected, but only when our relationship, connection, and communion with that land have been restored.

Conservationists have grown comfortable with our own success and ways of doing business, and are perhaps fearful of being pushed again to the margins of culture if we make too many demands. Conservationists rely heavily on donations of land and money from the industrial growth society and this makes us fearful of commenting upon the effects of that society. Some conservationists say commenting on culture will kill the golden goose. Others say that land conservation succeeds in America specifically because it doesn't tell Americans how to live, that it should keep its focus on buying land and not try to create social change.

It's true that conservationists need to keep their focus sharply on the land, but we must tell the story of how the land, and our relationship to it, can nurture a more just, happier, healthier society. We have to help others see how the well-being of each is dependent on the other. We've got to risk speaking the truth about how our disconnections from land and nature have contributed to massive cultural dis-ease. We need to risk being marginalized, as Rachel Carson was, to speak clearly for a different culture, one more closely connected to the natural world, even though this will be very difficult to achieve.

The facts tell why we must do this. The U.S. Department of Agriculture tells us that Americans are gobbling up the land at the rate of 365 acres per hour, or 3 million acres per year, *every year.* Conservation, on the other hand, has good years and bad but has not topped more than 2 million acres per year in land permanently protected. No, it's not likely that conservationists' goals can be accomplished purely through buying land, acre by acre. It is simply not possible, with today's far-reaching problems, to assume that any place on our planet can be protected *from* people. It can only be protected *with* people. We have to rely upon those landscapes to help all of us learn a new story about ourselves.

Saving land without speaking emphatically and bravely about the need for people to live differently only leaves the land vulnerable to our worst selves. For example, over the last twenty years, the land trust movement has saved 6.8 million acres of land. But are Americans more connected to the land than before? The fact that today there are more malls in America than high schools suggests not. What is the result? If we protect places of refuge without those places contributing to a new vision of how to be an American, the old American way of life will continue to destroy land faster than conservationists can ever save it.

This is a fateful time for the conservation movement. What felt thirty years ago to be quite radical—for example, the notion of conserving land by controlling development rights—is commonly accepted today. We've done good work. The dream of a network of land trusts across the country has exploded into 1,400 local organizations. Many of these land trusts have budgets in the hundreds of thousands of dollars while the national organizations have budgets of $50 million and more. Decades of hard work and growing successes have put conservationists more in the mainstream of culture than ever before. And yet, it's clear that the mainstream is an increasingly destructive force.

Perhaps it's time for the conservation movement to leave the comfort of our past successes and direct our formidable resources toward new solutions, new ways of thinking about our work. Nothing is harder to do because it means making new arguments and new friends. But many conservationists recognize that saving land alone is not a lasting solution to the crisis we're in. Many of us are skeptical of the enduring value of saving land without confronting the messy and complex struggle for the soul of our country. We sense that land conservation's great achievements would be leveraged many times over if through our work we could better convey the larger meaning of land and its importance in shaping an alternative American culture.

And just when we're beginning to feel secure and that we have lots of friends, this new work risks moving us back to the margins because it requires that we speak more of the truth and risk challenging and offending. This must be exactly what Rachel Carson felt before she started writing *Silent Spring*. But thankfully she was willing to marginalize herself by speaking an undiluted truth, and thereby advanced the quality of our life, our citizenship, and the health of our planet. Her fame and legacy—*the reason she is a hero*—is because of her courage to tell the truth.

How does land, and our relationship to it, change the way we think and act?

Today, the practice of land conservation becomes transformational to people and communities in both the process of *activism* and in the renewed *relationship* that a direct experience of the land affords people. The activism of saving land and the values and sense of care and belonging that develop around land open people to seeing the world with new eyes. In a world characterized by loss, inequity, and diminishment, to speak of one's love and to be able to protect it is always enlivening and hopeful. The opening of our hearts toward the fate of the land strengthens our emotional intelligence and refocuses us on our most deeply held beliefs. Almost twenty years ago, in his book *Biophilia*, E.O. Wilson concluded that human beings have an innate tendency to love and protect the natural world. This affection and affinity with the rest of life is apparently in all of us, buried under layers of cultural story, but brought to the surface fairly quickly by our ability to feel.

Anne and Bob Perschel, who combine a great understanding of our emotional intelligence with the motivations for wilderness protection, suggest that "our brains provide us with at least two guiding mechanisms. We have a rational brain that thinks and an emotional brain that feels." Our instincts and our ability to feel are affected tremendously by our relationship with the land. This is why what we do to the land—both good and bad—is forever shaping who we are. Anyone who doubts that we still get our fundamental cultural information from the land should drive out to the closest strip mall, stand in front of it, and ask themselves, what does this place say about me? How does this compare with how you feel when you walk in a healthy forest or see a healthy farm? What do those places say about you?

The American poet-philosopher, Frederick Turner, answers with: "all of us do have some kind of species knowledge of what it once meant to be connected. This knowledge is in our archaic brain stem and can never be expunged. It can be covered over. But it can never be erased. Whenever we come into contact with the natural world, it is awakened."

I have been part of dozens of conservation efforts where the emotional intelligence of people has been awakened by the activism of saving land and by their newly found citizenship. The acts of respect and forbearance toward land create a sense of membership with the rest of life that renews the human spirit. And this is what enables us to address other fundamental issues in our lives.

My favorite evidence of this transformational power of land conservation comes from the Nez Perce and the Trust for Public Land's efforts to reunite them with their home ground. It is a story of cultural and personal healing, which is to say it is about the human heart. The conservation project returned the Nez Perce to their ancestral grounds from which they were removed more than 125 years ago. One can quickly imagine the social value of this conservation effort to the Nez Perce people, but what did it ask of the white ranchers who had come to dominate this land since before the time of the Indian wars?

For a people who were forcefully removed from their land five generations ago, becoming a good neighbor requires a Herculean act of forgiveness. The return of the Nez Perce to their Precious Lands in 1997 somehow helped to inspire that forgiveness. Allen Pinkham, former chairman of the Nez Perce tribal council, spoke for his tribe when he said: "Returning to this land allows us to practice being good neighbors again. Our neighbors are the salmon and the eagle and the wolves and, yes, particularly the white ranchers and even their ancestors who killed our ancestors and drove us off our land. The land teaches how we must all live together as good neighbors."

The largely white community of Enterprise, Oregon, felt the same lessons and started thinking and acting differently because of the return of the Nez Perce. Many debated the appropriateness of the high school's mascot, the Savages, when the Nez Perce became the new neighbors in town, and they eventually decided to do away with the Indian caricature that adorned their building and basketball floor. The school board initiated a six-month community discussion about race, civility, and community life. Most remarkable, though, was their ability to then deal morally with one of the most difficult issues of the West: the control of water. The Nez Perce partnered with white ranchers and irrigators to reduce the amount of water flowing to farms so that salmon could be restored to the local rivers, an initiative that shares control of the river and makes neighbors out of salmon.

People, land, water, salmon. Fairness.

It's hard to describe what happened in Enterprise, Oregon, but one can feel that a different way of seeing and being emerged in the community. The act of conservation brought a people back to a land that was part of them, and others of a different race and ethnicity felt the desire to be whole again, too. In a short time, it became clear what was right and wrong and how to act from those convictions. Carla High Eagle of the Nez Perce explains this spirit as being the salmon itself:

> There is a promise you make when you're born to the Creator that says, "I will tell the truth. I will honor my family. I have a responsibility to the earth and to all those around me in everything that I do." The salmon is the same way. He was given instructions when he was born in the headwaters, and as he grew, that he would migrate down and he would be in the ocean and he would come back over the falls to achieve that purpose of coming back—to spawn and start the cycle of life over again—and his body would provide nourishment for everything that was there in the environment. That's the cycle of who you are. The land also recognizes and celebrates that same cycle. Every day. Coming home to the Precious Lands has enabled us to forgive and forget, to do what we must do as good neighbors.

This is social change. Mahatma Gandhi said that social change occurs when deeply felt private experiences are given public legitimacy. He added, "You must be the change you wish to see in the world." Gandhi led India with a model for social change that has been re-applied by Dr. Martin Luther King, Nelson Mandela and many others. Building upon these leaders' work as an activist during the nuclear disarmament movement, Joanna Macy began to describe the forces in our culture needed to create a "great turning" away from the industrial growth society to a life-sustaining society.

Macy describes the Great Turning as a gaining of momentum that happens simultaneously in three areas that are mutually reinforcing:

1. Holding actions that slow the damage to the earth and its beings
2. Analysis of structural causes and creation of structural alternatives
3. Fundamental shift in world view and values

We can see how Gandhi integrated all three. He directly confronted the oppression of British rule in India by enduring caning and arrest, and by creating ashrams and a new political party as a clear alternative to British rule. And he taught millions of Indians to weave their own cloth and to become more spiritually and materially independent.

The "holding actions" may be the most visible dimension of what Macy describes as the Great Turning. They include all the political, legislative, legal, and real estate work to slow down the destruction of the planet. This would include everything from defending the Endangered Species Act, to lobbying for the Land and Water Conservation Fund, to expressing civil disobedience toward anything that undermines social and environmental justice. Also, there are all the direct actions we take in our conservation work: the buying of land and defending of conservation easements to stop encroaching development or to expand wild lands or to preserve endangered species. Work of this kind is technical, heroic, wearing, stressful, confrontational, and buys time. We save individual special places, ecosystems, species, perhaps even some of the gene pool, but these acts are insufficient to create a turn in the direction of our society.

The second dimension of the Great Turning is equally critical. Macy describes it this way:

> We are not only studying the structural causes of the global crisis; we are also creating structural alternatives. These two efforts go hand in hand. They use the same mental muscles, the same kind of knowledge, the same itch for practicality. In countless localities, like green shoots pushing up through the rubble, new social and economic arrangements are sprouting. They may be hard to see at first, because they are seldom featured in the media. But if you keep your eyes open and fiddle with the focal length, they come into view like a faint green haze over things, intensifying here and there in pockets of green, cress, clover. Not waiting for our national or state politicos to catch up with us, we are banding together, taking action in our own communities. These actions that burgeon from our hands and minds *look* marginal, but they hold the seeds of our future.

This critical work includes the creation of new ways of describing and measuring the wealth and prosperity of our country, the spread of land trusts as an alternative form of land ownership for the commonwealth, local initiatives creating community gardens, community-supported agriculture, local currencies such as the Ithaca Dollar in New York, consumer and marketing cooperatives, educational efforts that help people to eat more locally and healthfully, efforts such as co-housing that make real alternative ways of living, and restoration projects reclaiming our rivers and brownfields.

These small and diverse efforts across our country are already having an effect, but they can not truly be linked together to take root without the presence of the third and most basic force in the Great Turning: a cognitive revolution and spiritual awakening. This is the lifting of the veil in order to see the world with new eyes. These opportunities come to us in many different ways: through our grief for the loss and diminishment in our lives or through our joy and hope in breakthroughs in science. In our endeavor of land conservation, we often foster these shifts in thinking just by giving a community a choice over the future of land. The activism of land conservation lifts the veil. We awaken to what we once knew: we are alive and in relationship with all other life. Macy describes the importance of this new way of seeing the world:

> These insights and experiences are absolutely necessary to free us from the grip of the Industrial Growth Society. They offer us nobler goals and deeper pleasures. They help us to redefine our wealth and our worth. The reorganization of our perceptions liberates us from illusions about what we need to own and what our place is in the order of things. Taking us beyond the tired old notions of competitive indivualism, they bring us home to each other and our mutual belonging in the living body of the earth.

Let's pause a moment and apply a similar process of whole thinking to land conservation. How is conservation already fostering these three dimensions of social change? How is land conservation aiding this ecological revolution or Great Turning?

The work of saving land is so difficult to begin with, how could we ever add these new dimensions of creating social change? The truth is that we're already doing it, but we need to make this part of the story of conservation much more explicit. Conservationists are transferring more than just legal title in each of our projects; we are transferring an element of power, hope, and self-determination to the people who are connected to that land. We are helping people to re-connect and re-imagine their lives. We need the words and the stories to make this meaning evident to more people.

Every land conservation project can and should be an enactment of a new vision of how to live. Conservationists can be educators by simply making more clear the motive behind protecting a piece of land and then encouraging the stories of that land to be told.

Conservation is fundamental to the ecological revolution because it's medicine for what ails our society. It has the potential to be much more than a holding action, or a Band-aid; it can offer a new vision for how we might better live, and be a source of personal transformation. We know this, and we have a moral responsibility to re-apply conservation in all ways that will enable it to create the change our planet needs. How do we get there?

The first step is to re-think the promise of land conservation as the promise of more enduring, healthy relationships. This will help us to evolve our work from being place-based to also becoming relationship-based. Second, we must be more explicit and courageous in speaking of conservation as a force of social change. Seeing our work as a force in creating a culture of conservation is difficult, and yet we are fully capable of it. This is how reformers show their radical hearts. This is the fusion between the radicals and the reformers. Many of us feel these things in our bones but can't yet articulate it: our intuition precedes the articulation.

Joanna Macy and her collaborator, Molly Young Brown, give us important direction in our time of intuition. They write, "Now in our time, these three rivers—anguish for our world, scientific breakthroughs, and ancestral teachings—flow together. From the confluence of these rivers we drink. We awaken to what we once knew: we are alive on a living earth, source of all we are and can achieve. Despite our conditioning by the industrial society of the last two centuries, we want to name, once again, this world as holy."

Most conservationists would agree, and would quickly remember a very similar feeling from their own experience. For example, because of her love of a mature forest in Greenwich, Connecticut, Louise Griswold left her private life behind and became an activist. She tirelessly talked to people and eventually created a coalition of over thirty organizations who agreed that it was important to protect a ninety-four acre forest that was destined to become a sub-division of homes. At the end of eighteen months of ceaseless effort, Griswold and TPL had found 1,400 people to contribute $11.5 million dollars to save the forest. Saving Treetops is less a story about raising money than it is a story about personal transformation. That forest changed a woman who went on to change many other people. Griswold describes it this way:

> I was part of something monumental, which I really can't understand but it gives me a great deal of hope for our community. I walk among the trees and say, "okay, I did it." I remember at one point my husband saying to me, "You act as if the forest has been waiting for you."

You can tell from the gray hair that I'm an old lady. So much has happened in the last few decades to shatter my idealism, and I did not want to end up being a cynical and bitter lady. I saw that appearances are deceiving, that things can be countermanded with enthusiasm and perseverance. It's exhilarating. Saving Treetops probably has been the experience of my life. People have been remarking how it's been so wonderful to see all aspects of this town working together. And it was interesting. We couldn't have saved it without the very wealthy who have their own estates and we couldn't have saved it without the rank and file. And person after person said saving this forest united the town.

Treetops is my sanctuary. This is where I come. This is my sanity. I'm thinking now that if this isn't a sacred place, it's coming pretty close. When you find a place like that, don't let it go.

This is an old and powerful story, an archetype of human life. Lifting the veil, we see anew the beauty and value in the world that surrounds us. Our humility in the face of this creation elevates our soul and helps us to take actions that both protect the earth while also restoring meaning and fairness to our lives. It is our re-entry into the world of life. It is the most courageous and transformational act of every one of our so-called environmental leaders from Muir to Thoreau to Leopold to Carson to Brower to Macy: renaming this world as holy.

Part 5. *Connecting Soul and Soil*

"Wildness and wilderness is determined not by the
absence of people but by the relationships between
people and place."

—Jack Turner

THE WIND OFTEN gathers below us in the Mad River Valley
and races up the pastures to grab the side of our barn as if it
were the mainsail of a schooner. Sometimes the blast rattles
the windows so ferociously I am sure they will blow out. But
more often it is a gentle, sustained exhalation that lifts the old
boards and twists every mortise and tenon just enough to make
me feel that I am on the water, riding the ocean swells. This
particular afternoon, the beams creak and groan slowly like an
old man breathing and this rhythm holds the eighteen of us
who are seated together sharing stories about our different
homelands. The breathing of this old barn and the stories it
helps us to tell remind me of the poet Barbara's Deming's
words: "our own pulse beats in every stranger's throat."

Our group of strangers has been together for only a day, but the
wind and this barn have slowed everyone down to a pace where
they can speak about what matters most. Each person has been
asked to bring an ordinary object from home that might help the
rest of us to better understand her. On the slate table in front of
us are the jaw bone of a deer, several stones of differing size and
origin, a medallion, a set of car keys, a pine cone, a butternut
shell, several snapshots of friends and family, a large piece of
kona wood, an etching of Gandhi, a book, and a bag of dark soil.
Each of these objects has come alive in front of us through the
telling of its meaning. A photographer from Seattle speaks of her
childhood love of a grove of willows that were cut down, and how
in her sadness, she wrote a young girl's letter to the author

Sterling North who understood and wrote back, "I weep for your willows." A conservationist from the Southwest fingers some yellow fiberglass insulation as he describes his concern about all the insulation we have brought into our lives. He asks us, "What are we insulating ourselves from?" An anthropologist from Michigan tells us a joke: "What's the difference between a developer and a conservationist? A developer builds homes in the wilderness and a conservationist lives in them."

We are a diverse group, though it is true that we are bound together by a professed love of the land. We are of many ages and colors and our activism has taken us to work in cities, in suburbs, in forests, in office buildings, and in remote corners of the world. We are writers, teachers, biologists, farmers, deal-makers, lawyers, philanthropists, and also mothers and fathers. Everyone remarks on the peculiar beauty and power of the table filled with random bits of wildness and memory. When our discussion is over, we leave the table exactly as is, sensing that its larger meaning has yet to reveal itself.

As our week together unfolds and there is time for reflection, some of the source of the power of that table becomes more discernable. First, we can see how a great many of the stories we have told are about places in our lives. Most of the objects have come from specific rivers, mountains, forests, or bays that have defined the person.

Even more profound, every story that was told and every object left on the table was about a relationship. We introduced ourselves through our connections to our lovers, our children, our religions, our dreams, our fears, the land. The stories that shape us, which we reveal when we need others to know what matters most, are about what we love, what we fear losing, what we have sorrow over having lost. Over and over again, we are defined by place and by relationship. Place and relationship. The experience of sharing those stories made real for each of us what Rachel Carson wrote in her introduction to *Silent Spring,* "even in the vast and mysterious reaches of the sea we are brought back to the fundamental truth that nothing lives to itself." We understand what D.H. Lawrence meant when he expressed, "in every living thing there is a desire for love, for the relationship of unison with the rest of things." We recognize, too, the fundamental truth that our own pulse *does* beat in every stranger's throat.

And as we discuss how we have translated our love of the land into our work for the land, it dawns on us slowly how our activism has treated place and relationship very differently, as if they could be separated. In fact, protecting a place has often come to mean restricting or stopping a relationship.

And with good reason. When Thoreau was living on the banks of Walden Pond there were one billion people living on Earth and now there are 6 billion. And collectively those 6 billion people have had an enormously destructive relationship with the land.

George Perkins Marsh was among the very first to raise concerns about the destructive impact of people to the land. Born in 1801, he grew up in Vermont during an era of vast changes in the land to accommodate sheep grazing. As a young man, he himself felled and cleared much forest which gave him the personal experience to conclude that human beings were "disturbing agents" of change. Marsh published *Man and Nature* in 1864 when he felt "there was no longer any place free from human influence." He wrote, "man, who even now finds scarce breathing room on this vast globe, cannot retire from the Old World to some yet undiscovered continent, and wait for the slow action of such causes to replace, by a new creation, the Eden he has wasted." This remains powerful wisdom, 138 years later, for a Vermont whose economy still relies on people leaving more urban homes to seek some mythical and idyllic new life in Vermont. Isn't it about time that we recognize our damage and begin anew a different relationship?

Our bad relationships have been seen everywhere. Now it's time to invest all of ourselves in proving that the good relationships are possible. In failing to do this what is left for us but to watch the clock?

Land is good for people, yes, but are people good for the land? We either glorify or demonize ourselves. The honest answer is that most of recent human history has not been good for the land. But there's also strong evidence of people yearning to live differently. When educated about alternatives and given choices, many Americans choose to act out of their human capacity for love, belonging, and for doing good.

The best evidence of this emerging ethical voice is seen at the ballot box. In the 2000 general election, Americans voted on 174 different land conservation bond measures around the country. These were local and state-wide elections where Americans were given the option to vote for higher taxes to raise public money to save land for open space and biological diversity. That year, when we had a very difficult time choosing our next president, Americans were resoundingly clear about their attachment to the land: 83 percent of those ballot measures passed. And this was not a one-time anomaly. In 1999, there were 92 land conservation measures, of which 90 percent passed. In 2001, there were 137 measures where 70 percent passed and in 2002 there were 141 measures, 75 percent of which passed. People want these lands protected and they want the relationship of these lands in their lives.

We can't throw out the people-land relationship; we've got to work to improve it. This is the great struggle of our time.

The symbol of this great challenge is the posted No Trespassing sign. In just two generations, the sign has sprung up everywhere from Vermont to Oregon. Today, there are many reasons to fear people coming on your land. There are problems with unwanted hunters, all terrain vehicles, hikers, bikers; you name it. Many people believe that they are best protecting their land by keeping people off it; for others, posting the land is just a more visible way of showing their ownership and rights.

Whatever the reason, more and more private land in America is posted and closed to people. And this phenomenon isn't just with private land, but also with land held for the public good by land trusts. Most land conserved by easements in America is not open to the public. And while this is surely helping some special places to remain healthy and untrammeled, it is also contributing to a culture less and less connected to the land.

Growing up in my own native New England, I saw very few if any of these signs as a child. I felt free to ride my horse through fields or to explore rivers that today are off limits. One now sees No Trespassing signs all over New England. It's true that all landscapes need to be respected and some need to be left completely alone, but in putting No Trespassing signs over so much of the land we have also put them across our souls.

In keeping people off our land, we may be momentarily protecting that place but shifting the problem to our neighbor's land. It's too late to shift the problem somewhere else; we've got to engage the real issue, which is our sense of ethics and the quality of our relationships.

When our direct human experience of the land is limited, our emotional intelligence is buried even further. We no longer see the shades of love that we once felt for the land. In "Speaking a Word for Nature," Scott Russell Sanders put the challenge very succinctly: "the gospel of ecology has become an intellectual one. For most of us, most of the time, nature appears framed in a window or a video screen or inside the borders of a photograph.

We do not feel the organic web passing through our guts. While our theories of nature have become wiser, our experience of nature has become shallower."

And the result is that our good relationships with the earth are increasingly made illegible or invisible. We work them to the margins while the bad relationships stay right in our face. We can easily blame the industrial growth society for all of these problems, but the truth is that conservationists hardly ever discuss examples of good relationships with place, relationships where people have taken the risks to live differently, more responsibly and closer to the land. Those who do live by that love of the land feel more and more that they are lone voices. Why has the conservation movement allowed these good relationships to be overshadowed by the bad relationships?

One answer is that in our need to compete effectively in the world of politics, finance and real estate, we've become more technical and less emotional. We have come to value our proficiency *in* the tools of our work more than our relationship *to* the source of our work.

In the past, we have honored the good relationships and made them the symbols of our movement. We love Thoreau's relationship with Concord, John Muir's relationship with the Sierra high country, Mardy and Olaus Murie's relationship with the Brooks Range, Harlan and Anna Hubbard's relationship with the Ohio River, Aldo Leopold's relationship with Sand County, Helen and Scott Nearings' relationship with their homesteads in Vermont and Maine. There's something deeply inspiring to us whenever people develop a connection to the land that leads them to change their own lives and reach their fullest potential. There's something there that many of us yearn for. And yet today's conservation movement has little to say about that relationship and so few new stories. There are so many organizations, and so few stories of how to be.

When we ask ourselves today what are the deeds of great conservationists, one might speak about the passing of new laws
and the protection of the remaining wild and evocative landscapes. These deeds are heroic and critical and we can't stop
doing them, but we also need the poetry and example of healthy
human relationships with the land. The stories we can tell about
good relationships with the land resonate with all humans as
loudly, as courageously, and as joyfully as anything else we conservationists could ever legislate, negotiate or protect.

This is Richard Nelson's relationship with the Tongas, Terry
Tempest Williams' relationship with Red Rock Country,
Charles Wilkinson's relationship with the Colorado Plateau,
Gary Nabhan's relationship with the Sonora Desert, Julia
Butterfly Hill's relationship with an ancient redwood. And it's
the thousands of as yet untold stories of stewards of the land—
field biologists, farmers, urban gardeners, young ecologists,
foresters, environmental historians—whose kinship with a
place has re-defined their lives.

Some land trusts and national conservation organizations are
re-imagining the power of these human relationships. They are
re-thinking all the ways that people access the natural world
and then seek to keep open those doorways, which include
recreation, an appreciation of aesthetics and beauty, a source of
human spirit and inspiration, the desire for intellectual knowledge, and also food and work.

Some conservation organizations are partnering with community-supported agriculture and other local food networks to
help people feel more connected to the land three times a day
through eating healthy, local food. Food helps people commit to
the process or cycle that produced it. For example, when we eat
from local farms, we commit ourselves to those places. When
we eat from organic fields, we commit ourselves to healthy
soils. When we eat wild salmon, we commit ourselves to

healthy rivers. When we shoot and eat a deer, we commit ourselves to healthy forests. When we eat factory-raised poultry
and meat, we commit ourselves to factories.

Others are working in cities to show, ever so clearly, that city
dwellers can have a close relationship to the land that is about
more than a place to jog. Urban life need not compete with
nature or with country life. Our cars, power grids, industries,
and buildings can all be more a part of the process of life. We
know through biomimicry and two-thousand-year-old innova-
tions in architecture how to design and live this way. Cities are
where we can close the gap between the natural world and our
world.

Still others are opening their lands to loggers, farmers, and
fishermen who have a special intelligence of their own and
who can help us create new and contemporary models for living peacefully and healthily on the land. Other organizations,
like TPL, are working closely with tribal governments and
native peoples to restore their traditional uses of the land. All
of these groups, in their own ways, have had an epiphany:
their own veils have been lifted, to see that the only enduring way to protect this earth is through helping people to re-
connect.

This "connecting land and people" philosophy for conservation seeks the restoration of all the sets of relationships—
human and nonhuman—that is called the land. If we can
inspire conservationists to aim their work toward the rebuilding
and protecting of those relationships, we will have helped conservation to become a social movement and to create a much
greater shift in culture.

Thinking of land conservation as the conservation of relationships defeats the illusion of separation in our lives. The
two core ideas to help us re-think the promise of land conservation are these:

1. We can't save land through our separation from it, but only through our sense of belonging *to* it.
2. The focus of conservation ought to be on the restoration of enduring relationships—human and nonhuman—to create a land that is a unified whole.

Re-thinking land conservation as the promise of more enduring relationships is like seeing our world with new eyes. And this new worldview can create changes in our culture as important as any in the history of our species, because it enables conservation to be more than holding actions, to become an enduring source of alternative models of living and a source of the personal transformation that is the fertile ground for broader shifts in culture.

Our struggle over land is particularly transformational because it's ultimately about love and loss and healing. It's about relationship. And most people get this, without having to know all the science, because we humans—at our core—are more tuned to connection than to isolation. Conservation must appreciate and respond to this depth of human need for belonging.

Everything we do, every tool we use, ought to focus equally on the land and on the opportunity for fostering that human belonging: the interdependencies between people and place, between people and one another, between people and species, between the human world and the more-than-human world.

Initially, it's as simple as asking ourselves in every conservation project:

> In what sense are we restoring our own relationship to this land?
> How can our health and the health of this land be improved?

What do we hope to learn from our own relationship
   to this place?
What are the stories from this place that we want to
   bring to our community?
What does this place teach us?

Because most people's relationships to the land are purely
economic, it's particularly profound when we can highlight
relationships that are not about money. This means protecting
the good examples of the way people live, which is much more
difficult than protecting the land itself. By the mere fact of our
global impact, every single human living today has a connection
and a relationship to the land that ranges somewhere from
exploitation to kinship to complete forbearance. We need not
see or touch that land for the effects of our relationship to be
felt on it. Our life in Vermont, for example, can create landfills
in Kentucky, dam rivers in Canada, and cause old growth
forests to be cut in the Olympics. Our way of life has enormous
negative impact on wild lands everywhere. This fact leads critics to say that all this talk about relationship as a guiding prin-
ciple for conservation neglects our fundamental need for vast
landscapes that must be left alone to be self-willed.

What does our human need for relationship say about wilderness? Wilderness will only be allowed to remain when humans
can act with tolerance. Wilderness will be respected not only
because it has been legislated by an act of Congress but
because we define our connection to that place through our
love and forbearance. The health of a wild ecosystem becomes
the standing, living definition then of our capacity for self-con-
trol, restraint and mercy. These are powerful characteristics of
relationship, too.

What are the natural habitats that humans need most to survive? What makes this question complex, more complex say

than understanding the habitat needs of the grizzly bear, is our species reliance on both what we are given and what we make, our dependence on both nature and culture. We are just beginning to understand that there are "land- and people-scapes" that are especially evocative because they strike powerful emotional and physical responses in people.

A land-and-people philosophy of conservation focuses on protecting places that inspire *querencia,* or a sense of belonging. These landscapes clearly define a sense of home, express people's shared sense of cultural identity, and bond people to one another and to the land itself. In the Southwest, it's the acequias, in California it's access to the beaches, in New England it's healthy coastline and estuaries as well as the health of small scale farming and forestry. It's protecting the places that we have a birthright to, that help us find our roots or put down new roots, enabling us to envision the land as part of ourselves.

Be they farm, lake, mountain, or historic site these places are "charismatic," in that people gravitate to them unconsciously, often for hundreds of years before they are threatened. They often have a long human history, and those stories from the past help to orient people and connect them in the present. The ability to witness "history in nature" brings people and that land into a shared timeline.

These are places whose significance comes from the merger of land and people and story. They aren't necessarily spectacular or rich in biological diversity. They can be a little bit of green on the edge of town, and still resonate profoundly.

These are often landscapes that inspire a commitment to social justice and the great need to bring the experience of the natural world to children and families who have little opportunity to experience the land. These are landscapes that inspire our childhood remembering: local, common places where people often had their first direct experience with the natural world. As one elderly native Californian said while drinking in the view from the top of Vulcan Mountain near Santa Barbara, "This is like the Old California I knew when I was a kid!" The desire to re-connect with that experience is profound within all of us. And when those childhood landscapes are destroyed, we accelerate the detachment and the acceptance of loss in our lives.

Important, too, are the landscapes that remind us daily that our relationship with the land is also about work and sustenance. Farms, oceans, rivers, forests. These are landscapes where people struggle to provide the food and wood that all of us rely upon. These places connect people to local traditions and cultures and sources of food. These are the places in the natural world that many Americans perceive as their "community life." These landscapes are evocative and pierce into our consciousness, positively and negatively as healthy forests or clear-cuts, because they reflect our everyday struggle to live in balance. Lived upon with wisdom, these landscapes help us to re-define the meaning of progress. It's critical for the conservation movement to know that there are many more Americans who earn their livelihoods in the forests and fields than there are members of conservation organizations. Both sets of connections to the land are rich, valuable, and worthy of protecting.

There are also the landscapes that serve as important reminders of how much the world is changing. These are a community's "last" landscapes: the last working farm in town, the last public swimming hole, the last bit of unplowed prairie, the last traditional fishing community, the last old-growth forest. They are symbolic of our changing times, but not entirely nostalgic. They can stand as positive reminders of another way of living.

There are landscapes that remind us that our connection to the land has helped us to achieve a greatness that isn't about money and power. These are sacred and symbolic landscapes that have helped people to find their own source of inspiration. They are evocative because they challenge or affirm the way people think and act. Creating a national park to honor Martin Luther King, Jr. and protecting the threatened lands that inspired Thoreau interject critical questions into our lives: What is the connection between civil rights and the environment? How might Thoreau's notions of civil disobedience inform and guide how we live today?

There are landscapes that remind us that we are animals, still completely dependent upon the health of our habitats. These are the landscapes that provide for our clean water, air, and food.

The most remarkable feature of these modern times is not that we are on our way to destroying the wealth of the earth— that's old news. It's that we're beginning to wake up to a whole new set of relationships to our world and to ourselves. It's time that we take a new pledge of allegiance. A pledge about what we will and will not accept in our lives. A pledge that reflects that our eyes are now open, that we can see, that the veil has been lifted.

Part Six: *Whole Thinking*

"My teaching is a raft whereon men may reach the far
shore. The sad fact is that so many mistake the raft for
the shore."

—Siddhartha Gautama, Buddha

I HAVE BEEN cleaning the kitchen floor of our old farmhouse.
I have swept and mopped this floor countless times, though it
still shows the wear of many years of living. This week we will
touch, lift, and polish much of our life as we ready to welcome
friends and family to our hilltop farm. If someone washes the
floor, someone cleans the windows, someone cuts flowers from
the garden, someone cleans the chicken coop, someone mows
the fields, will this farmstead be clean? My objective in wiping
clean these old windows is not to let in an unobstructed shaft
of sunlight, but to prepare myself for our wedding, and to show
our love, as best we can, for ourselves and for our friends and
family who will gather here. We want to create an orderly place
to live where we might be free and healthy to pursue the larger
dreams in our lives. I wipe this old window as best I can without the expectation that I can get it truly clean.

When the Buddha said, "the sad fact is that so many mistake
the raft for the shore," he was pointing out the very common
problem of confusing means with ends. Am I laboring over this
old house to get it clean or to achieve some larger objective?
This is also a critical question for land conservationists. What
is our raft and what is our distant shore?

The raft is *how* we get to the distant shore, but the shore is
why we are rowing in the first place. My guess is that many
conservationists would say that the purpose of their work is to
save land, to protect the biodiversity of the planet, to maintain
local economies closely connected to the land, to expand our

system of wilderness areas, and to control and reduce sprawl. These are all critical and noble objectives, but are they a means or an end? Are they the shore, or in doing them are we trying to achieve something even more promising? Can we further articulate our motivations for doing each of these things?

When we take the time and effort to fully consider and explain our intentions, we come closer to understanding the values that motivate us. By holding those values up closer to the surface of our work, we stand a better chance of realizing them. We stand a better chance, also, of attracting others to us. When we fail to speak of the larger purpose of our work, and we row without our destination firmly in mind, eventually we become lost. And if we're lost long enough, we confuse the raft for the shore.

One reason why more Americans don't vote or act more consistently the way environmentalists would hope is that environmentalists are always talking about the raft as opposed to the shore. And, frankly, that raft is a scary place to be. Rowing it is hard work: it's out in the middle of a rough sea without a clear destination. How many people are likely to buy a ticket for that trip?

Many more people share environmental values than want to be called environmentalists. Why not, then, avoid the labels and stick with the values? We use the labels so often because we can't express the values. Using labels is further evidence of our confusing the raft for the shore.

The marketers of our consumer culture do not suffer these confusions. They feed Americans a very simple story about 30,000 times a year in the form of commercial advertisements: buy this product and you will be healthier, wealthier, sexier, more secure, have more fun, and be more successful. The distant shore is made to sound very close and alluring. No wonder our heartfelt pleas to live differently so often fall on deaf ears.

• • •

What is land conservation's larger purpose, what is the distant shore to which we are rowing? We might have many different answers for this. Here are some of mine: we save land in order to slow the diminishment of our human lives and the lives of all other things on this planet. We conserve land because we do not accept the illusion that the fate of humans is in any way separate from the fate of salmon, or bald eagles, mollusks or liverwort. We conserve land because land is where our relationship with the rest of life, our fundamental happiness and security, is proven. We save land to make real for people the respect we feel for one another. We save land because it is in our relationship with the rest of life that we find enduring meaning and joy. We save land because it's far more fun, healthy, sensual, and enriching to live in a whole world.

Why do we fail to speak more often of these larger purposes? There are good reasons why it has been hard for conservationists to think and act in an integrated way. One answer is the specialization of our organizations. The environmental movement of the 1970s evolved very quickly into technical, highly specialized corporations because that focus gave them the skills and resources to compete quickly within the existing system. They thought they needed to look like the opposition in order to compete. It's nearly impossible, though, to see the big picture when you're working on a small corner of it. In highly specialized organizations, big picture values look fuzzy and out of reach.

Specialization has given us important tangible achievements. It has enabled us to pass many critical laws and to protect millions of acres of land, but hasn't helped average Americans to trust one another enough to dwell and imagine their lives differently. It hasn't given us an integrated philosophy of how to live well. *To live well* means to care for the land as the only enduring way to care for ourselves. The "good life" in America has come to mean something almost exactly the opposite: that our security and wealth and happiness come primarily from our bank accounts and not from our relationship with the world around us.

We can't compete our way into an ecological revolution. But we can offer people, through each and every one of our protected lands, a different view of the world that is healthier, happier and more realistic than the one our dominant culture would have us believe in.

Whole thinking is the only way out of the specialization box, the only way to create a culture of conservation that can address questions such as: What matters most, how do we want to live, and how do we get there together?

Whole thinking is viewing the world through the lens of kinship and integration. It speaks to ecological truths, that the world of life is connected, not separated. It takes responsibility for the whole: linking cultural diversity and natural diversity, fusing civil rights and environmental rights, showing that the health of big wilderness is directly connected to the health of our core cities. It speaks to cultural truths, that our tolerance toward the land is tolerance toward one another. A kindness toward one another would be false if it were surrounded by a neglect for the land, just as it would be a troubling deceit to find protected land where there is not fairness among people. Whole thinking enables conservationists to begin to connect the whole landscape, from cities to wilderness, and from ethnicities, races, social classes, and generations to endangered species.

The land is a unified whole, and human communities are inseparable from this unity, so our activism needs to be holistic. The effort to work across the full spectrum of habitats, from inner city to wilderness, is an expression of this determination to think about and bind together the whole land community.

Gary Nabhan, the accomplished ethnobotonist from the Sonora Desert, points out the critical importance of Whole Thinking to the protection of biodiversity:

> Conservationists have again and again tried to build an "ark for biodiversity." Like Noah, they have been willing to usher along every kind of plant and animal as long as no other peoples are given a place aboard the ark, forgetting that until the very moment of crisis, a diversity of cultures served to safeguard that biodiversity. The Huaorani, Tukano, and Zapara have not been offered berths to ensure their own survival. Conservationists have given them little place in their plan except as Bystanders, allowed to watch as all the animals go two by two up to higher ground.

Integrating Whole Thinking into the daily work of land conservation requires a constant balancing of three tensions, all of which are based on an ethos of relationship and restoration:

1. Valuing process and place
2. Protecting subject and object
3. Holding the how and the why

Holding the tension that exists naturally between these forces is complex work. It's so much easier to release the tension and simply go back to the specialization and polarities that have characterized the conservation movement. To struggle to hold these tensions, however, is the mark of our mature and compassionate leadership, one that stands a chance of telling a new and more compelling story to Americans. It is how we might finally achieve an environmentalism of mind, body, land, and soul. One that defeats the illusion of separation.

Valuing process and place is the act of recognizing that at least two distinct things are going on when we protect land. We are protecting a physical place and we are initiating a process of re-connecting humans to that place. The process of conservation, when grounded in tolerance and fairness, has the ability to transform people, and to prove our greater citizenship. In this light, conservation is not place-based but relationship-based.

Protecting subject and object is recognizing that elements of our own identity and future are in the land we are trying to protect. In thinking of land as both object and subject, we are also defeating the inclination of all organizations to treat land, though bought and sold, as a commodity that is separate from living creatures including ourselves. In viewing land as both object and subject, we also stand more of a chance of evolving our role as observer of the natural world to a participant in it.

No one describes this tension better than Pierre Teilhard de Chardin, who in the last century applied Whole Thinking to scientific research and religious vocation. At an early point in his career this paleontologist and Jesuit priest made it his personal mission to reconstruct the most basic Christian doctrines from the perspectives of science and, at the same time, to reconstruct science from the perspectives of faith. He wrote:

> Almost incurably subject and object tend to become separated from each other in the act of knowing. We are continually inclined to isolate ourselves from the things and events which surround us, as though we were looking at them from outside, from the shelter of an observatory into which they are unable to enter, as though we were spectators, not elements in what goes

on . . . it did not occur to the first evolutionists that their scientific intelligence had anything to do in itself with evolution.

Holding the how and the why is the most powerfully creative and exciting tension of all. It is our ability, as conservationists, to match our great technical skills with the ability to hear and re-tell the story of the meaning of the land. Conservationists bring so much hope to communities when we can save land, and this is our chance to also bring meaning and purpose.

How We Conserve Land	Why We Conserve Land
Focus on our tools	Focus on what those tools accomplish
As opportunities arise	Planned to fulfill mission goals
Number of acres saved	Lessons learned, communities changed
Specialized technicians	More broadly focused leaders
Changing real estate title	Creating a land ethic in people
Buying land	Telling stories from that land
Recognizing a change in the land	Recognizing a change in people
Creating hope	Giving meaning

How will we balance these tensions and bring these ideas into the daily work of land conservation? There are many ways, and two of the most promising are storytelling and re-defining how we measure our success.

Stories, especially stories about our connection to place, are like oxygen. They keep us alive and awake. Telling stories is the best way to help people feel the importance of land in their lives. Stories explain the meaning of conservation through metaphor and analogy, not just fact. They elevate our emotional intelligence without degrading our rational intelligence. They re-mystify and renew our spirit toward the land just at a time when conservation has become largely about legal agreements and financial structures. Everyone loves stories, and so they stand the best chance to change the way we think and act.

The Center for Land and People has published a handbook on storytelling (*The Story Handbook,* 2002) that can help all conservationists to recognize, listen for, and tell stories about the land. Our conclusions from that book are that every conservation project has the opportunity to teach people to see the world differently, to dwell and imagine their lives differently. Every conservation project can quietly confront mainstream culture with a different story about what life was meant to be. Every conservation project can offer people the example of a healthy relationship, a more meaningful connection, with the rest of life.

Learning to tell stories starts with learning to hear them. Here are examples of the elements of stories that we can hear from the people who are connected to a place, and that we need to learn how to retell:

- Stories that reflect our highest aspirations, that show our values
- Stories that show another way of being human
- Stories of hope and possibility
- Stories that show our love and commitment to the diversity of life
- Stories that tell fundamental truths about the world we live in
- Stories of how we would like the world to behave
- Stories that include the wholeness of the human condition, that don't shy away from emotion, conflict, sorrow, joy, love, memory
- Stories about the history of our cultural ideas and practices, our ancestry

- Stories that merge the land and human community
- Stories that are humble, that do not preach
- Stories that give a voice to people who are less
  often heard
- Stories of people feeling that they are part of a solu-
  tion, not part of the problem
- Stories about reclaiming the commonwealth, about
  economics that favor the health of the land

Every conservationist knows that these rich stories tell a much more complete picture of the values and benefits that arise from connecting people and the land. These speak to the true success of land conservation, even though it is hard to describe and harder still to measure. Falling back on counting acres and dollars, however, throws us quickly into the trap of focusing on the raft and not the distant shore.

How might we re-define conservation success in terms of building relationships? I can only share the learning that we are doing at the Center for Land and People. We have begun the long process of working with fellow conservationists, writers, educators, sociologists, and many others to understand how we might better measure our conservation effectiveness based on how conservation creates a change in the health of people and the land together. Thus, and most importantly, we are helping to extend the philosophy of conservation biology to include the habitat needs of people. The beginning of that learning is charted at the end of this book, in "Whole Thinking in Practice."

Fifty years ago, Aldo Leopold wrote "there are two things that interest me: the relationship of people to each other, and the relationship of people to the land." What's vitally important about this statement is that Leopold was thinking deeply about both people and land. He was part biologist and part sociologist or, more likely, he saw little distinction between biology and sociology. He understood the nutrient cycles of the soil and the integrated, holistic nature of the ecology of life. And he knew that people need a natural habitat in order to maintain healthy bodies, hearts and souls. Leopold saw the health of people and the health of the land as inextricably linked in a dance of hope and sorrow.

The most meaningful and enduring stories from many cultures across the world speak directly to this dance of hope and sorrow between people and the land. And the story often goes like this: No one knows for sure how they settled here, but for thousands of years, they lived stable lives shaped by the chemistry of the soils, the animals that lived around them, and the mysteries of the stars. Their lives changed little and their traditions evolved slowly in response to patterns of living that lasted generations upon generations. It is inevitable, the story reveals, that this life could not go on unchanged forever. And so change does come, and for some it is blisteringly quick and for others it is slow and insidious. But, at one point or another, the story ends the same way: the people break their connections with the land. They are lulled into different lives by far-flung economies, by having their land stolen from them, by lies told on television, by desires unnamed to their hearts. There are so many different ways to leave, but always one conclusion: their lives and their myths are broken.

Sometimes, it takes a child to bring them back. An innocent who can still hear the stories in the wind, who can act out of love before the veil is lowered. She gives them the opportunity to re-write the ending. We love this story because it speaks truthfully of the sorrow of our disconnections, and yet remains hopeful for the future. We all have within us that innocent child who can envision a new story and then work to make it become our reality.

Whether you work in the forest, in the fields, in an office

building, with a hammer, with a hoe, with a pen, or with a microscope, this life asks you to be awake. This life asks that you engender affection as well as knowledge and wealth. This is the way we might free ourselves from this culture of isolation to create an alternative culture of meaning and connection.

PETER FORBES is director of TPL's Center for Land and People, a farmer, photographer, and the author *The Great Remembering*, another title in this book series on conservation and culture.

WHOLE THINKING IN PRACTICE

AT THE TRUST for Public Land, we have developed a rubric for describing and measuring conservation projects based on their alignment with five overall mission objectives and their ability to deliver eight social benefits that our organization highly values. We envision that the indicators of these values and benefits will be greatly improved and expanded upon by hundreds of conservationists, until one day, years from now, we have a new framework for guiding and measuring the success of land conservation in terms of building healthy relationships between land and people.

Values that the Center for Land and People seeks to promote through land conservation:

1. Thinking about the whole

When conservation takes responsibility for the whole, from inner city to wilderness, it speaks biological truths, serves to connect landscapes, and educates people about critical inter-dependencies. A whole natural system, including humans, is what conservation ought to protect.

2. Protecting what people love

Conservation should highlight people's shared values and their local passion for what they know and love. This brings people together and helps them fear one another less. By protecting what people love, we offer a positive vision of the world we want to live in.

3. Integration of healthy land and healthy people

Conservation is about economic, mental, physical, and spiritual well-being. It's often about healing ourselves and other life.

Through this view of life as one healthy whole, restoration of land and of oneself become the same.

4. Striving for fairness

Conservation's impact becomes more profound as it serves all people, regardless of income, color, or where one lives. Everyone needs and deserves a relationship with the land. Similarly, it is fair and moral for conservation to honor the gift of all life, not just human life, and to respect the life, health, and independence of many ecosystems.

5. Honoring home

By focusing on where people live, work and play, conservation protects the places that enable us to think about who we are and where we belong. It roots us, and helps us to better value and appreciate the places immediately around us. The work of local conservation provides the daily reminders that what we do to the land, we do to ourselves.

We can enhance our ability to nurture and deliver these values within a community by evaluating the following **benefits,** one or more of which can result from each conservation project.

1. Care-Taking and stewardship

Each piece of land we protect serves a rich natural and cultural set of objectives, and we know, through research, the sustainable uses needed to maintain the health of that land for the foreseeable future. With funds perpetually in place to maintain the land and a diverse cross-section of the community committed to ongoing stewardship, such a conservation project leads those involved to take care of other lands. Through wise stewardship, the property is restored or improved.

2. Teaching and storytelling

The story of the conservation of this land expresses values that are fundamental to who we are as a people.

The lesson from the conservation of this land teaches a story about conservation or about the meaning of the land itself that is shared among many people in the community. The land, itself, is an enactment of another way of living that creates a powerful and convincing narrative about healthy land is vital to human well-being in many ways.

The story is unique and compelling, so that it moves people to consider their lives differently. The story is told in many communities beyond where it originated.

3. Cultivating connections to nature

There are widely recognized natural and cultural values on this land that can be experienced by people either as direct experience on the land or as intellectual or personal inspiration from afar. Human use or experience of this land improves its health. Conservation of this land promotes a diversity of ways that people might experience nature: through recreation, work, food, aesthetics, and beauty, through human spirit and renewal, and through intellectual knowledge. By providing people with the direct experience or indirect inspiration of the land, we can help them understand the needs and realities of the larger ecosystem, thereby encouraging them to consider and take responsibility for the whole.

The natural experience associated with this project is unique, yet a diverse spectrum of people is able to have this experience.

4. Fostering responsibility for the whole landscape

Our vision for conservation considers the whole landscape from parks for people, to working lands and wild lands. We are committed to taking on many different projects, all of which conserve different places and ecosystems within the whole landscape. Our conservation efforts across the spectrum of habitats help people to integrate and connect these different places. For example, a farmers' market in a core city helps people to understand the value of forests and farms.

This conservation project connects people to a variety of landscapes, creates a human sense of empathy for the rest of life, and nurtures tolerance and a broader view of the world.

5. Healthy habitat for communities

We are protecting a large landscape that plays a very important role in purifying air or water quality for a community or region. We are remediating hazardous wastes that posed a threat to the community. We are "undeveloping" land to remove structures that created environmental problems.

A single project creates awareness of the need for conservation on a larger scale to protect environmental quality. This conservation project, because of its scale or location, is critically important to public health and safety for an entire community or region, such as protection of a sole-source aquifer.

Our action has a major impact on public policy that strengthens leaders to protect or create a healthy habitat for humans.

6. Healthy habitat for individuals

A significant cross-section of the community will benefit from better opportunities for recreation, relaxation, and improved mental health. Playgrounds are being created for schools so that children have healthier environments. Lands being protected are used to instruct people in healthy ways to exercise, eat, and live.

Our work cleans up hazardous waste and reduces toxins that affect human life. Our conservation efforts revitalize a human culture by restoring a link to the land that promotes community-wide physical and mental health.

This project creates a visible model for improving health that influences foundations and governments to devote more resources to parks and land conservation.

7. Civic engagement

This project helps a community become more self-aware. The act of conservation galvanizes the community to better understand itself, work together, shift political structures, and create significant new social capital. The standard of citizenship is raised as more people rally around a common conservation cause, and thus the public sphere is expanded, and opposing forces are brought together in healthy debate about a wide range of issues. The community recognizes the connection between parks or land conservation and other fundamental issues of life such as education, justice, and common welfare.

This conservation effort avoids a change in land use that would have broken important community bonds.

8. Justice and fairness

This conservation project is making significant progress in correcting inequities, for example by:

- helping an Indian tribe regain the use of lands that are important for cultural or economic purposes
- adding parks in low-income neighborhoods that fall below minimum standards for access to parks

This conservation project creates change within the community, by building support, fostering institutions, or generating resources that have widespread beneficial impacts on justice and fairness. This conservation effort redresses a widely perceived injustice and is widely recognized for its significance.

This conservation effort leads to a meaningful and lasting change in policy by governments, foundations, or NGOs to promote justice and fairness in access to parks and conservation lands.

Our work illustrates the fundamental human respect for nature. This project elevates what it means to be human by addressing our sense of fairness toward all life.

A LAND AND PEOPLE INDEX

Researched and compiled by

CARA ROBECHECK

1. Number of acres the US loses each **year** to sprawl: 3,200,000

2. Number of acres the US loses each **day** to sprawl: 8700

3. Number of acres the US loses each **hour** to sprawl: 362.5

4. Percentage change in the population of the US from 1982 to 1997: + 17

5. Percentage change in the urbanized area of the US from 1982 to 1997: + 47

6. Acres of prime farmland lost per year to development from 1982-1992: 400,000

7. Ratio of farmland being saved through conservation measures to farmland being lost to development: 1:3

8. Amount of money brought in by nature-oriented tourism annually in the US: $14 million

9. Percentage of the US population that enjoy some kind of wildlife related recreation: 77

10. Percentage of California's threatened and endangered species for whom sprawl is detrimental: 66

11. Acres of lawn in the US: 20,000,000

12. Pounds of pesticides used on US lawns in 1994: 32,000,000

13. Ratio of the likelihood that a child will develop acute lymphoblastic leukemia in homes were lawn and garden pesticides are used compared to those where they are not used: 6.5:1

14. Number of commonly used lawn pesticides that are linked to birth defects: 14

15. Percentage of US summer air pollution that comes from gas-powered lawn equipment: 5

16. Ratio of water runoff from a paved acre to water runoff from a one-acre meadow: 16:1

17. Gallons of water lost annually to runoff in Atlanta that would infiltrate through natural surfaces: 132,800,000,000

18. Number of people whose household water needs could be supplied by the amount of water lost annually to runoff in Atlanta: 1,500,000

19. Percentage of water-impervious surfaces in suburban areas that are transportation related: 60

20. Number of vehicles in use in the US in 2000: 230,957,227

21. Ratio of miles traveled by car in 1990 to miles traveled in 1970: 2:1

22. Percentage change in highway congestion for each 10 percent increase in the highway network: + 5.3

23. Percentage change in civic engagement for every 10 minutes of daily commute: -10

24. Number of US fatalities and pedestrian deaths each year from cars: 46,000

25. Since 1905, 250 million people have been maimed or injured in car accidents, and more have been killed than in all the wars in American history.

26. Number of motor vehicles for every 1000 Chinese citizens: 8

27. Number of motor vehicles for every 1000 Americans: 750

28. Number of miles of new road laid down in Florida each day: 2

29. Ratio of pollution emitted by SUVs and light trucks compared to a standard car per mile: 2.5:1

30. Percentage of the world population that is American: 4.7

31. Percentage of greenhouse gas emissions created by Americans: 25

32. Year since which Americans have used up more resources than everyone who ever lived on Earth before them: 1950

33. Number of countries in the world that spend less on everything they buy than Americans spend on trash bags alone: 90

34. Pounds of material that are mined, extracted, wasted and disposed of to provide an average American middle-class family with its needs for a year: 4,000,000

35. Ratio of time spent shopping to time spent playing with their kids for the average American: 7:1

36. Number of hours per week an average American 12-year-old spends exposed to commercial messages: 48

37. Number of hours per week an average American 12-year-old spends conversing with his/her parents: 1.5

38. Ratio of shopping centers in the US to high schools: 2+:1

39. Worldwide, ratio of money spent on advertising to money spent on education: 2+:1

40. Annual amount that consumer spending increases for each weekly hour of TV viewing a person averages: $208

41. Hours of TV watched by Americans in 1996: 250,000,000,000

42. Number of square feet of retail space per American: 27

43. Money spent by candidates for US federal office per registered voter: $9

44. Money spent per American on National Parks each year: $6

45. Number of planet Earths that would be needed if the world population consumed resources at the rate that the US does: 4

46. Cost of providing a basic education to all people in the world: $6,000,000,000

47. Amount of money spent each year on cosmetics: $8,000,000,000

48. Percent of US streams and lakes that are too polluted for swimming or fishing: 40

49. Minimum amount of water the average person needs to survive per day: 1.3 gallons

50. Minimum amount of water a person needs for drinking, cooking, bathing, and sanitation per day: 13 gallons

51. Average amount of water used daily by a person in the US: 65-78 gallons

52. Average amount of water used daily by a person in the Netherlands: 27 gallons

53. Average amount of water used daily by a person in Gambia: 1.17 gallons

54. Percentage of Earth's forests that have been disturbed or destroyed: 80

55. Percentage of US forests that have been disturbed or destroyed: 98-99

56. Acres of rainforest destroyed each second worldwide: 2.5

57. Percentage of worldwide wood harvest that Americans consume: 27

58. Pounds of paper used annually by the average American: 700

59. Percentage of paper that is recycled in the US: 45

60. Number of the 10 warmest years on record that have occurred since 1989: 8

61. Percent that the arctic ice has thinned since 1989: 40

Index Sources

1. USDA Natural Resources Inventory 12/2000

2. USDA Natural Resources Inventory 12/2000

3. USDA Natural Resources Inventory 12/2000

4. "Paving Our Way to Water Shortages: How Sprawl Aggravates Drought," by Betsy Otto, Katherine Ransel, and Jason Todd, *American Rivers;* Deron Lovaas and Hannah Stutzman, *Natural Resources Defense Council;* John Bailey, *Smart Growth America.*

5. "Paving Our Way to Water Shortages: How Sprawl Aggravates Drought."

6. "Once There Were Greenfields: How Urban Sprawl Is Undermining America's Environment, Economy and Social Fabric," by F. Kaid Benfield, Matthew D. Raimi, and Donald D.T. Chen (New York: Natural Resources Defense Council, 1999.)

7. "Once There Were Greenfields: How Urban Sprawl Is Undermining America's Environment, Economy and Social Fabric."

8. "Once There Were Greenfields: How Urban Sprawl Is Undermining America's Environment, Economy and Social Fabric."

9. "Once There Were Greenfields: How Urban Sprawl Is Undermining America's Environment, Economy and Social Fabric."

10. "Paving Paradise: Sprawl's Impact on Wildlife and Wild Places in California." A Smart Growth and Wildlife Campaign California

White Paper, National Wildlife Federation, February 2001.

11. "Counter Culture," in *Grist Magazine,* from 50 *Simple Things You Can Do To Save The Earth. See Grist Magazine* http://www.grist-magazine.com/

12. "Counter Culture" in *Grist Magazine,* from the EPA.

13. VPIRG quoting a National Cancer Institute Study. See http://www.vpirg.org.

14. VPIRG

15. "Counter Culture" in *Grist Magazine* from National Wildlife Federation.

16. *America's Rivers.* See http://www.amrivers.org.

17. "Paving Our Way to Water Shortages: How Sprawl Aggravates Drought," by Betsy Otto, Katherine Ransel, and Jason Todd, *American Rivers,* Deron Lovaas and Hannah Stutzman, *Natural Resources Defense Council,* John Bailey, *Smart Growth America*

18. "Paving Our Way to Water Shortages: How Sprawl Aggravates Drought."

19. "Paving Our Way to Water Shortages: How Sprawl Aggravates Drought."

20. Glickman, 2001

21. "Once There Were Greenfields: How Urban Sprawl Is Undermining America's Environment, Economy and Social Fabric."

22. *Affluenza,* by John De Graaf, David Wann, and Thomas Naylor. Berrett-Koehler; 2001.

23. *Bowling Alone,* by Robert D. Putnam. Simon & Schuster, 2001.

24. *Affluenza*

25. *Affluenza*

26. "Counter Culture" in *Grist Magazine,* from World Resources Institute.

27. "Counter Culture" in *Grist Magazine,* from World Resources Institute.

28. "Counter Culture" in *Grist Magazine,* from National Wildlife Federation.

29. "Counter Culture" in *Grist Magazine,* from the *Los Angeles Times.*

30. *Affluenza*

31. *Affluenza*

32. *Affluenza*
33. *Affluenza*
34. *Natural Capitalism,* by Paul Hawken, Amory Lovins, and L. Hunter Lovins. Boston: Little, Brown and Company, 1999.
35. *Affluenza*
36. *Affluenza*
37. *Affluenza*
38. *Affluenza*
39. *Environmental Ethics Today,* by Wenz, Peter S. New York: Oxford University Press, 2001
40. *Environmental Ethics Today.*
41. *Environmental Ethics Today.*
42. "Harper's Index" *Harper's Magazine,* September 2002.
43. "Counter Culture" in *Grist Magazine*
44. "Counter Culture" in *Grist Magazine*
45. UNEP. See http://uneptie.org.
46. UNEP
47. UNEP
48. *Affluenza*
49. People and the Planet. See http://www.peopleandplanet.net.
50. People and the Planet.
51. People and the Planet.
52. People and the Planet.
53. People and the Planet.
54. "Counter Culture" in *Grist Magazine,* from Natural Resources Defense Council.
55. "Counter Culture" in *Grist Magazine,* from World Resources Institute.
56. "Counter Culture" in *Grist Magazine,* from Natural Resources Defense Council.
57. "Counter Culture" in *Grist Magazine,* from Natural Resources Defense Council.
58. "Counter Culture" in *Grist Magazine,* from Environmental Defense Fund.
59. "Counter Culture" in *Grist Magazine,* from World Watch Institute.

60. McKibben, Bill. "How Much is Enough? The Environmental Movement as a Pivot Point in Human History." Speech at Harvard Seminar on Environmental Values, October 18, 2000.

61. McKibben, Bill. "How Much is Enough? The Environmental Movement as a Pivot Point in Human History."

FOR FURTHER READING

Abram, David. 1996. *The Spell of the Sensuous*. New York: Pantheon.

Berry, Wendell. 2000. *Life is a Miracle*. Washington, D.C: Counterpoint Press.

———. 1981. *Recollected Essays 1965–1980*. San Francisco: North Point Press.

———. 1992. *Sex, Economy, Freedom and Community*. New York: Pantheon.

———. 1995. *Another Turn of the Crank*. Washington, D.C: Counterpoint Press.

Bookchin, Murray. 1982. *The Ecology of Freedom*. Palo Alto: Cheshire Books.

Carson, Rachel. 2002. *Silent Spring*. Boston: Houghton-Mifflin. (Originally published 1962.)

Cronon, William. 1995. *Uncommon Ground*. New York: W. W. Norton.

Deming, Barbara. 1974. *We Cannot Live Without Our Lives*. New York: Grossman Publishers.

Diamond, Jared. "To Whom it May Concern," *New York Times Magazine*, December 5, 1999.

Dillard, Annie. 1982. *Teaching a Stone to Talk*. New York: Harper and Row.

Drucker, Rabbi Malka. "A Jewish Time Capsule," www.malkadrucker.com.

Ehrenfeld, David. 1993. *Beginning Again*. New York: Oxford University Press.

Eisenberg, Evan. 1998. *The Ecology of Eden*. New York: Alfred A. Knopf.

Eldridge, Niles, "A Field Guide to the Sixth Extinction," *New York Times Magazine*, December 5, 1999.

Fischer, Peter. 2001. *The Great Remembering*. San Francisco: The Trust for Public Land.

Forbes, Louis. 1950. *The Life of Mahatma Gandhi*. New York: Harper and Row.

Freeman, Martha, ed. 1995. *Always, Rachel*. Boston: Beacon Press.

Freyfogle, Eric. 2001. *New Agrarianism*. Washington, D.C.: Island Press.

———. 2000. "A Sand County Almanac at 50." *ELR News and Analysis*. Washington, D.C.

———. 1998. *Bounded People, Boundless Lands*. Washington, D.C.: Shearwater Press/Island Press.

Hartmann, Thom. 2001. *Last Hours of Ancient Sunlight*. New York, Harmony Books.

Hogan, Linda. 1995. *Dwellings*. New York: W. W. Norton.

Jensen, Derrick. 1995. *Listening to the Land*. New York: Context Books.

———. 2001. *The Culture of Make Believe*. New York: Context Books.

Kellert, Stephen R. 1997. *Kinship to Mastery: Biophilia in Human Evolution and Development*. Washington, D.C.: Island Press

Kemmis, Daniel. 1995. *The Good City and the Good Life*. New York: Houghton Mifflin.

Kunstler, James Howard. 1993. *The Geography of Nowhere: The Rise and Decline of America's Man-Made Landscape.* New York: Simon and Schuster.

Leopold, Aldo. 1986. *A Sand County Almanac.* New York: Ballentine Books (New York: Oxford University Press, 1966).

Macy, Joanna. 1991. *World as Lover, World as Self.* Berkeley, California: Parallax Press.

————. 2001. *Widening Circles.* New Society Press.

————. 1998. *Coming Back to Life.* New Society Press.

Marsh, George Perkins. 2003. David Lowenthal, ed. *Man and Nature.* University of Washington Press. (Orginally published in 1864.)

Meadows, Donella H. 1991. *The Global Citizen.* Washington, D.C.: Island Press.

Moore, Kathleen Dean. 1999. *Holdfast.* New York: Lyons Press.

Nabhan, Gary Paul. 1997. *Cultures of Habitat.* Washington, D.C.: Counterpoint Press.

Nash, Roderick. 1989. *The Rights of Nature.* Madison: University of Wisconsin Press.

Nearing, Helen, and Scott Nearing. 1954. *Living the Good Life: How to Live Sanely and Simply in a Troubled World.* New York: Shocken Books.

Pollan, Michael. 1991. *Second Nature.* New York: Atlantic Monthly Press.

Saltmarsh, John. 1991. *Scott Nearing: The Making of a Homesteader.* Chelsea Green Publishing.

Sanders, Scott Russell. 1998. *Hunting for Hope.* Boston: Beacon Press.

————. *The Country of Language.* 1999. Washington, D.C.: Milkweed Editions.

————. *The Force of Spirit.* 2000. Boston: Beacon Press.

Servid, Carolyn. 2000. *Of Landscape and Longing.* Washington, D.C.: Milkweed Editions.

Snyder, Gary. 1990. *The Practice of the Wild.* San Francisco: North Point Press.

————. 1995. *A Place in Space.* Washington, D.C.: Counterpoint Press.

Teilhard de Chardin, Pierre. 1965. *The Phenomenon of Man.* New York: Harper and Row.

Thoreau, Henry David. 1958. *Walden.* New York: Harper Classics (Boston: Houghton Mifflin, 1854).

Turner, Jack. 1996. *The Abstract Wild.* Tucson: University of Arizona Press.

Watts, Alan. 1951. *Wisdom of Insecurity.* New York: Vintage Books.

Wilkinson, Charles. 1999. *Fire on the Plateau.* Washington, D.C.: Island Press.

ABOUT THE CENTER FOR
LAND AND PEOPLE

How can we make conservation more effective, not only for preserving land but also for nurturing community? While we have saved millions of acres, Americans seem less connected to the land than ever before. Our best hope is to work for a shift in American culture. By inviting citizens to imagine their lives differently, by offering them new ways of dwelling in the land, we can help replace the culture of exploitation with a culture of conservation.

The Center for Land and People works to create a greater understanding of the many benefits that flow from a respectful relationship with the land: human health, ecological health, economic sustainability, enriched community life, companionship and fairness between humans and with other species, and the renewal of the human spirit. By linking changes in the land with changes in people, we seek to enlarge the impact of conservation, carrying it beyond the measure of acres and dollars—important as those are—to the measure of social and individual well-being.

We conserve land because of core values including respect, justice, generosity, compassion, the desire for belonging, and love. Land conservationists can expand these values into culture by revealing them more courageously and explicitly in each project. We encourage this through our programs, which include: helping conservationists to redefine success for the movement, creating forums for deeper conversations about core values, encouraging storytelling as a vehicle for change, convening dialogues between diverse members of the land community, and publishing a series of books on "Re-thinking the Promise of Land Conservation."

For more information about the Center for Land and People or the Trust for Public Land, visit www.tpl.org.

The Center for Land and People's
Rethinking the Promise of Conservation Series

Our Land, Ourselves
Readings on People and Place
ISBN 0-9672806-0-5
240 pages, $16.95

The Great Remembering
Further Thoughts on Land,
Soul, and Society
ISBN 0-9672806-1-3
112 pages, $14.95

The Story Handbook
Language and Storytelling
for Land Conservationists
ISBN 0-9672806-2-1
100 pages, $14.95

*Coming to Land
in a Troubled World*
ISBN 0-9672806-9-9
144 pages, $16.95

All of these titles can be ordered from your local bookstore, or from Chelsea Green Publishing Company. Call 1-800-639-4099 or find them online at: wwwchelseagreen.com.

For a complete list of publications from the Trust for Public Land, go to www.tpl.org.

This series is funded by the Educational Foundation of America, the Nathan Cummings Foundation, the Compton Foundation and the Park Foundation.